FORD: A VILLAGE IN THE
WEST HIGHLANDS OF SCOTLAND

FORD

A VILLAGE IN THE WEST
HIGHLANDS OF SCOTLAND

A Case Study of Repopulation
and Social Change
in a Small Community

John B. Stephenson

with the assistance of Sheena Carmichael

PAUL HARRIS PUBLISHING

Edinburgh

First published in Great Britain by
Paul Harris Publishing
40 York Place
Edinburgh
© Copyright John B Stephenson 1984

ISBN 0 86228 081 8

*The publishers acknowledge the financial assistance of
the Scottish Arts Council in the publication of this book*

Typeset by Jo Kennedy, Edinburgh
Printed in England by Billings & Sons Ltd.

Contents

Acknowledgements

So many people have helped with this book that another volume would be required to thank them all adequately. The people of Ford are, of course, owed the greatest debt because of their interest, generosity, and patience in sharing their accustomed realities with an unforgiveably naive stranger. Sheena Carmichael is acknowledged on the title page for her special role in providing books, letters, photographs, and other historical materials, in accompanying me on brief but important excursions into the Mid-Argyll area, in allowing me to test half-formed impressions and rewarding me with the most kindly of corrections and admonitions, and in reading the manuscript carefully several times. Perhaps as important as all this practical assistance is the fact that Sheena imparted to me her unbounded affection for the Mid-Argyll district.

Special thanks are also due David Murray, Sr., and to David and Amy Murray, who, along with Sheena Carmichael, shared what they had and without limit what they knew. And to Maimie and Dempster and Eddie and Margaret and Hamish and Jean, Alec MacDougall and Major William Warde-Aldam and all the rest— although I cannot name all of them here, I hope they will feel my gratitude.

I am indebted greatly to Robin Malcolm of Poltalloch, who set me straight on many matters dealing with agriculture, local government, family history, Scottish society and culture, and local lore. I still have much to learn, but the task is made easier thanks to his good-natured tutelage.

Ronald Baird, Bridge of Allan, was likewise most generous in his explanations of current agricultural practices, policies, and problems. Roy Campbell, Murdo MacDonald and especially the late Eric Cregeen were indispensable sources of advice and information regarding West Highland history.

In Stirling, Dorothy and Donald Anderson were among those who simply made life possible for us during this stay in Scotland, quite beyond the contribution of their frank critiques and appraisals as the manuscript took shape. Alison Bowes is also owed thanks for her encouragements.

7

I was more than fortunate that Alex Coupar, Dundee, a family friend of Sheena Carmichael, was able to furnish photographs for the book. His excellent work will be found between pages 80 and 81. (The others are my own.)

Thanks go to my wife, Jane Ellen, and to Francene Nash, my staff assistant in Kentucky, for preparation of the manuscript, and to my daughter, Rebecca, for careful proof-reading.

This study was made possible through a Senior Research Fellowship from the Fulbright Programme on a leave supported by the University of Kentucky and its Research Committee.

Finally, I wish to thank Sir Kenneth Alexander, Principal of the University of Stirling and former Chairman of the Highlands and Islands Development Board, for his willing help throughout the entire project.

My characterization of Ford, its past and future, would be considerably impoverished without the help of all those acknowledged here. The final result is my own, however, and I must take full responsibility for its errors and shortcomings.

John B. Stephenson
Lexington

List of Illustrations

14 Ford Bay of Loch Awe. Once the site of the pier used by loch steamers putting into Ford, Ford Bay is now used mainly by anglers. (AC)

15 *Cnoc an Ath*, the burial mound across from the Ford Hotel. Unexcavated and unmarked, its significance is nonetheless known and respected by villagers. (JBS)

16 Tree-planting in Inverliever Forest, about 1964. Donald MacCallum, brother to the Postmistress, is on the left. Ronnie Mathieson and Robert Gillies are in the background. The Forestry Commission still provides work for a number of men in the village, as does private forestry. (AC)

17 Houses in 'The Row'. All but the rightmost house have been built since the late 1960s and are occupied by incomers. (JBS)

18 Known as the Crown House or the Change-House, this is one of the oldest structures in Ford. Tired horses were changed for fresh ones in the days when the drove road was used heavily. John Keats is said to have stayed the night here while on a walking tour of the West Highlands. (JBS)

19 This old manor house at Ederline Estate is said to have been built in the eighteenth century. It is occupied by the estate gamekeeper; the estate owner lives in a modern house built in the 1960s. (JBS)

20 Duntrune Castle, home of Robin Malcolm, 19th Laird of Poltalloch. The foundations of the castle are Norman, dating from the twelfth century. (JBS)

21 Creaganterve Farm, with an ancient standing stone near the original Glennan Farm site in the foreground. (JBS)

22 Schoolhouse at Ford, with the school attached at the rear. It has been used as a private residence since the school closed in the 1970s. (JBS)

23 Mr MacKinnon with sheep on Torran Mor Farm. (AC)

Photographs marked (AC) *by Alex Coupar
and those marked* (JBS) *by the author.*

Preface

The case for welcoming the publication of a new book dealing with the Highlands and Highland problems is certainly not that such books are rare events. The case for welcoming this book is that the quality of perception and understanding it brings to the examination of the social life of a small Highland community is quite exceptional when measured against the standards achieved in most of such studies. This quality has been achieved firstly by concentrating on a small and reasonably distinct community, secondly by bringing to the work a personality and related attitudes which minimise the risk that what is related has been much influenced by the very presence of a researcher, thirdly by the experience of the author in comparative studies in another remote area of a developed nation and fourthly by the modesty and caution shown by the author in making his points and in drawing conclusions.

The book would be difficult to classify, and this is a strength. Social history, sociology, anthropology, antiquarianism, rural development? All approaches and certainly all aspects are to be found here. Naturally the particular skills of the rural sociologist have been deployed by an author who directs a highly reputed centre for such work, but neither the theory nor the methodology is obtrusive, and the reader is allowed to concentrate on the real matters in hand – how a community has developed and is developing, and the patterns of living currently to be found within it.

Against the background of my own concern for development in the Highlands and Islands, what I find most valuable in the study is the extent to which it sees its community, Ford, as dynamic rather than static, with its movement and change substantially generated internally, that is, self-generated. It is very easy to see Highland communities as static, becalmed in a wider society which is experiencing dramatic social and economic change. Despite the constraints on his time and of space to set out all that he learned in the confines of one book, Dr Stephenson does not present us with a snapshot of Ford, or even with a succession of snapshots, but gives us the picture of a community in motion.

11

That, coupled with the extent to which this study in depth explores the complexity of the relationships and factors which are producing this change, makes this book not only of interest to the general reader who wishes to understand such community life but of great value to those concerned with the administration of the Highlands, administration being interpreted widely to embrace the range of institutions and professions at work in the region. Simplistic models of cause and effect are quickly seen to be inadequate and quite probably misleading, despite the temptation to construct and use such models in the mistaken belief that small scale communities lend themselves to such an approach. Dr Stephenson lays no claim to being a 'social engineer' and his work should prove a valuable corrective to those whose inclinations lean in that direction.

Dr Stephenson is careful to emphasise the distinctive character of Ford – a particular illustration of the general point that the Highlands is made up of a large number of distinctive communities and that it should not be assumed that it is safe to generalise from one such to the other. The Highlands is not one homogeneous region; although there are some common problems there are fewer common solutions.

At the University of Stirling we were very pleased to have the Stephensons as part of our community, and there is cause for further pleasure that Dr Stephenson's time with us has been so well spent in the production of this excellent study of another small community in Scotland.

Kenneth Alexander
August 1983

To the Memory of

Alasdair Carmichael
Ford's native writer

and

William Stephenson,
An emigrant from Donegal
to the New World in 1732

'The chiefs of other times are departed.
Another race shall arise.'

Ossian

1 Introduction

*Of the many inherited visions of the
Highlands, which is the reality?*
Hugh Quigley
The Highlands of Scotland

I have a very simple purpose in writing about the village of Ford: to
share what I have learned about the nature of life in the rural West
Highlands of Scotland today. It is more than idle curiosity which
drives me to seek this understanding and to share it. Growing
mainly out of a lifelong attachment to the central Appalachian
region of the United States and a concern with its future, this
interest has become more general over the years and encompasses
a concern with the fates of remote communities everywhere. As
technological improvements in communication, information-
handling, and transportation encourage the further centralization
of commercial and political interests, life in the countryside is
increasingly at the mercy of decision-makers located in distant
cities. There is much to be learned about the life and death of small
communities through the study of their histories, their rounds of
daily life, and what is happening to their populations, whether they
are located in the Blue Ridge Mountains of the United States or the
Highlands of Scotland. Perhaps with the accumulated knowledge
from such studies from around the world we can determine what
forms of adaptation lead to vitality in peripheral human communities.

Aside from this long-range cumulative concern, the West
Highlands of Scotland are interesting for their own sake. There is a
considerable 'literature' about the Scottish Highlands, much of
which is of the tourist variety which decorates coffee tables outside
of Scotland. Some of the romantic fog has been penetrated by

15

writers such as James Hunter and John Prebble, who have shown us a version of history which goes far beyond the 'Balmorality' promoted by Queen Victoria and Sir Walter Scott. But reliable accounts of life in the rural Highlands today are not plentiful, despite the fact that numerous social scientists are said to be working currently throughout the region. I was able to find only one community study situated anywhere in Scotland published in book form: Professor Littlejohn's *Westrigg, The Sociology of a Cheviot Parish*. This study was published in 1963; the research was conducted some years earlier. There appear to be almost no books or monographs published from community studies or general ethnographies in the mainland Highlands.[1] The published and unpublished work carried out by anthropologists and sociologists seems to be concentrated in the Western Isles (as in Judith Ennew's *The Western Isles Today*), in the Shetlands and Orkneys, and in the Cromarty Firth-Inverness area, or generally where oil developments have had greatest impact.

The reading public, as well as social scientists, therefore suffer from a major gap in what has been published about the Highlands. This is a remarkable discovery, given the strong popular interest in the Highlands, and given the vigorous tradition of community study in other parts of Britain (numerous examples of published studies come to mind from Ireland, England, and Wales). While one small book representing a single village study cannot pretend to fill this gap, this volume is intended to be a small contribution and a source of encouragement for others to come forth with better and more extensive work. As knowledge of life in the contemporary Highlands accumulates and becomes available to the public, the region will become, one hopes, more than just a kind of scenery, more than a piece of dead history wrapped in tartan.[2]

There are two central themes or ideas around which this book turns. One, as suggested, is the question of the future of the village of Ford: Will it survive, or will it die? The other, not unrelated to the first, is the somewhat surprising fact of the re-peopling of the village within the past few years. All the rest is history, prologue, backdrop, but it is essential to the issue of the village's life or death and to an understanding of the importance of repopulation.

One of the starkest features of Highland history is the loss of its people and the disappearance of its communities. The remains of croft dwellings, estate mansions, and castles can be seen in a number of places; in many glens there is simply nothing at all to remind today's visitor of the scores of inhabitants who once lived there. The bleeding off of the population of the Highlands has continued for so long that it is taken as a fact of life by many of those who remain, as well as by many of the newcomers who choose to live there. In the course of the first conversation I held with anyone in the village of Ford, I asked, 'What kind of place is Ford?' The answer was, 'Ford is dying, like a lot of other places that have gone before it. In a few years there will be nothing here but the remains of houses, just like the ghost villages you can find up the road.'

I accepted this observation (or prophecy) as a reasonable representation of the truth. Indeed, in the course of my early visits to Ford, I found evidence to support an unfavourable prognosis. The prospect of documenting the demise of the village was not something I relished, but the facts seemed to point to slow death. Or did they? Gradually, I began to shed the preconceptions of some of my informants and see certain other facts more clearly. The most important of these facts was that the population of the village was increasing, not declining. The recognition of this fundamental fact, reinforced by reading Rosemary Lumb's report, which confirmed that in-migration was occurring in certain other Highland villages, led to a series of related questions: Who are the newcomers? When did they come? From what places did they come? What effects are they having on social life and culture in places like Ford? What bearing does their presence have in predicting what kind of future lies ahead for the village?

In understanding the past, present, and future of Ford, it is important to know what kind of community it is and is not. It is a very small line village laid out on a secondary rather than a main road. It began somewhat inadvertently (unlike certain other, planned villages in the Highlands) as a crossroads community no later than the early eighteenth century, and probably earlier. Its people are farmers, foresters, labourers on estates, and caterers to travellers and tourists. The occupations held by villagers today are incredibly diverse, as we shall see.

Ford is not a town, and some would say that it is not a true village, but rather a 'hamlet', which means that in the views of some who know the place, it is relatively small, weak, and unimportant in comparison to larger, main-road villages which somehow have more 'definition'. Places such as Oban, Fort William, and Lochgilphead are thought of as true towns. They are sub-regional centres of transportation, commerce, and government. Nearby Kilmartin and Kilmichael are thought of as villages, sometimes in contrast to Ford, partly because they are located on a more important road.

Unlike some other types of Highland communities, Ford is not a village which was planned as part of an estate, nor has it ever been located entirely on a single estate, although, as we shall see, its history has been heavily influenced by neighbouring estates. The fact that it is not and has never been tied to an estate distinguishes it from places such as Cairndow and Slockavullin, also located in Argyll.

The story of Ford may also be different from those of certain other West Highland villages because it does not serve a single industry. While it has been an important place for travellers from its beginnings, it is not simply and solely a tourist village such as those which virtually fold up in the winter and come back to life like the gorse in the spring. It likewise is different from fishing villages, and from industry-dominated villages such as those near the slate quarries at Ballachulish, the erstwhile pulp and paper mills near Fort William, or any of several hydroelectric plants. Nor is it affected much by the oil developments which have taken place largely on the other side of the country.

Ford is not located in a crofting area of the Highlands, and its history, if not its present and future, was undoubtedly influenced by this fact. Argyll once enjoyed numerous crofts,[3] and some still exist on the islands and in northern Argyll, but they began to disappear in this section of the Highlands at a much earlier time than elsewhere. It does not appear that anything like a 'crofting community' coalesced on the mid-Argyll mainland in the fashion which Hunter describes farther to the North and West.[4] Exactly what difference it would have made had Ford been a crofting village is not known, but it is said that crofting communities are closer-knit than non-crofting communities. And while it is perhaps no less likely that lands would have changed hands in a crofting area as newcomers moved in and native residents left, the actual use of the land would have changed less because of the regulations and policies of the Crofters Commission.

Recognizing what Ford is, and what it is not, will help in placing limits on what we can claim to know about Highland villages from looking at this one place. To study a community is to use it as a window through which to look at the rest of the region, a country, or the world, but one cannot see everything through a single window. How extensive are the patterns described in Ford? How far should one generalize to other kinds of communities and other areas of the Highlands? I really cannot say with certainty. The findings of Rosemary Lumb suggest that Ford is not alone in experiencing the effects of incomers and in losing many of its native working-age people. But all the evidence is not in, and I wish to be cautious in making claims about what is known, especially because I am a foreign newcomer myself. Readers will extrapolate as they see fit.

My investigation into the life of Ford took place in the autumn of 1981, when I enjoyed the support of a Fulbright grant-in-aid to be in residence at the University of Stirling as a Visiting Research Fellow. I conducted extensive interviews with residents of the village as well as with others outside the community who knew it from different vantage points. Observation of life in the village supplemented these interviews in invaluable ways. I had considerable library work to do, not only in locating historical references to Ford and Kilmartin Parish, but in filling in the great void in my knowledge of Scottish history, politics, economics, and geography.

The sun was shining on my first visit to Ford. I did not know how rare an event this was until much later. On this day I made a great, looping trip northwestward from Stirling, through Crianlarich and Taynuilt to Oban, then southward to Lochgilphead and westward to LochLomondside and Dumbarton back to Stirling, leaving the main roads to drive through numerous small places in the hills in search of villages which might be candidates for study. I picked up a hitchhiker in Crianlarich. In his sixties, Charley Boyle was a Donegal man who had emigrated to Scotland when he was very young; he had worked in many of the places through which we passed. In exchange for the free ride, Charley offered a running commentary on the area as we drove through it, and he listened patiently (or slept) as I argued out loud why this place was too large, that one too small, the other one too dominated by tourists to be suitable for my purposes, which he never completely understood. No matter, Charley and I both liked Ford when we drove into it. I left the car and walked around for a few minutes, and then chatted to one of the residents. She could not think why anyone would want to write about Ford, but neither could she think why anyone would object. When I resumed my journey, I said to Charley Boyle, 'I can't say why exactly, but I think this is the place.' Charley agreed politely that it was a nice little village. (You're not likely to read this, Charley, but thank you for your company and for your lessons in geography, regional and national attitudes, and pronunciation.)

Of the roughly twenty villages I explored briefly in this fashion on this and another trip farther east, Ford came back to my consciousness more frequently than any other. I went back a second time and took my wife to help explore further. We liked it, and the people we met there seemed to accept us and the idea of a study. It was on this visit that we met Sheena Carmichael, who eventually became a collaborator in the investigation, helping with the historical materials and a census of the community, and gently correcting my interpretations of local events and culture. Ford was the proper size for my purpose, it had a mixed economy, and it was the right distance from my base in Stirling. But I also confess that I felt at home there, and that this feeling of acceptance and attachment influenced the decision to choose it as an object of study. In looking back on my good fortune, I realize that on that first day the sun was shining in more than just a literal sense.

The feeling of acceptance continued throughout the period of my stay in Ford. I made no attempt to disguise my purpose in being there. Nor have I made any attempt to disguise the village or its people—a decision reached after consultation with a number of them: they would prefer to be revealed as themselves (or as I see them) than to be fictional or anonymous. I have taken the additional step of sharing drafts of the manuscript with several of the people of Ford so that I can benefit from their correction and reproof. The final product is more truly collaborative than anything I have written before, and I believe it is a better document for that reason.

There were some advantages and some disadvantages to being an outsider—and an American—in Ford. The major advantage was that I could ask embarrassingly naive questions without engendering surprise or dismay among my friends in the village. They educated me about a number of matters which I am certain they had always taken for granted themselves. I think all of us came to be more analytic and more sensitive to social and cultural patterns which made up community life through this process. Had I been native to the area, I would have run the risk of taking these patterns for granted myself.[5]

On the other hand, the foreigner is often so naive that he risks missing the point of things altogether; I hope I have minimized this possibility by involving some of my informants as participants in the study. There is also a great cost in the time required for an outsider to learn the history and background of an unfamiliar area which is necessary to put the present in the proper contexts. While I have tried to read extensively and to converse with knowledgeable parties wherever I could come across them in Scotland about local history, politics, government policy, nationalism, international markets, the EEC, agricultural practices, forestry, emigration, unemployment, regional economic development strategies, and so on, nevertheless, there is much more to learn than I now know.

This 'report' from Ford is written not only for an audience of social scientists, but for general readers as well. It is intended to inform anyone who wants to understand what life is like in the rural West Highlands today, who wants to know some of the historical circumstances from which the present has emerged. It is also intended for reading by both Americans and Scots. There are hazards in attempting to write for all these audiences simultaneously; by writing 'in the middle', the message may fall short of everyone for whom it is intended. But there is so much to be gained from looking closely at the nature of life in small places such as Ford. This picture of life in the West Highlands may appear less romantic than most American readers will have imagined; if so, it will serve as an appropriate and overdue corrective. To Scottish readers, much of what is said here may appear self-evident. If there is nothing new here, then at least we can lament the fact that no one before has taken the trouble to make it a part of the available ethnographic record.

But I believe strongly that there are things we can all learn from Ford—and from all the Fords of the world. I am driven to share my new knowledge of this, the place I came to understand and love. I would urge any student of humanity to do likewise.

The following chapter briefly describes the geographic setting and the economic bases of the village of Ford. Chapter 3 includes a more lengthy historical sketch of Ford and the area surrounding, including the three estates which played roles in its history. Chapter 4 is a rather straightforward narrative description of life in Ford today as a social scientist would view it. In Chapter 5 the theme of repopulation is developed in the context of the prior history of depopulation. Some of the consequences of repopulation are examined in this section and the nature of the incoming population analysed. The final chapter returns to the opening question, 'Is Ford dying?' and examines the evidence against a background discussion of vitality and death in communities in general. The conclusion is a tentative and qualified 'No'. Ford is not dying. It is changing. Whether Ford, and other places like it, continue to live and change depends as much on decisions and events far removed from this locality as on anything the people of the village do to save it, as vitally important as those efforts are.

Footnotes

[1]One exception to this conclusion is the important paper by Dr Rosemary Lumb entitled 'Migration in the Highlands and Islands of Scotland' (Institute for the Study of Sparsely Populated Areas, Research Report No. 3, University of Aberdeen, October 1980). This report includes valuable current demographic information from ten Highland communities along with thumbnail sketches of the communities, one of which is in Argyll. Unfortunately, the existence of this report is not widely known.

[2]Neil McCallum, *It's an Old Scottish Custom* (London: Dennis Dobson, 1951).

[3]Crofting is a complex of legal rights and culture patterns pertaining to smallholdings traditional to parts of Highland Scotland. The crofter rents his smallholding from a landlord for a price set by the Scottish Land Court. Buildings and other improvements are his, not the landlord's; tenure on the land is secured by the right of inheritance and the right to assign use of it to another party for payment (subject to approval of the Crofters Commission). For decades, in the majority of cases, the income from crofting has been supplemented by other, non-agricultural earning. See James Shaw Grant, 'Crofting', An Comunn Gailhealach publication No. 10, Inverness, 1976); Katherine Stewart, *Crofts and Crofting* (Edinburgh: William Blackwood, 1980); Crofters Commission, Annual Report for 1980 (Edinburgh: HMSO, 1981).

[4]James Hunter, *The Making of the Crofting Community* (Edinburgh: John Donald, 1976).

[5]This and kindred issues are discussed at length in John B. Stephenson and L. Sue Greer, 'Ethnographers Studying Their Own Cultures: Two Appalachian Cases', *Human Organization*, Vol. 40, No. 2 (Summer 1981).

2 The Setting:
Ford and the Mid-Argyll District

*It is to the west that people go if
they take their mountains, like their
whisky, with a little water.*
Neil McCallum
It's an Old Scottish Custom

Argyll is that section of the Scottish Highlands which is the most
southwesterly. Although it was one of the original seven crofting
counties, a fact which places it historically in the tradition of the
clanship system, use of Gaelic, and the institution of the croft itself,
Argyll's proximity to Lowland Scotland has placed it in a marginal
position between the Highlands and Lowlands. It stretches roughly
from the River Clyde on the south to the area called Morvern north
of Loch Linnhe. Argyll includes the Island of Mull on the north and
the Kintyre Peninsula to the south. For almost three hundred years
Argyll was controlled by the families of Clan Campbell, first as
Earls, then as Dukes of Argyll.[1]

Almost fourteen hundred years ago when the Irish successfully
invaded what is now Scotland, they entered the country on the
coast of Argyll, which takes its name from a Gaelic word meaning
'the coast of the Gael'. The three sons of the invader, Erc, were
given dominion over three different sections of the new territory.
The area of Argyll known as Lorne, which includes that part from
Loch Linnhe to Loch Awe, is named for Lorn, son of Erc. The more
southerly part of this sub-area of Argyll is sometimes referred to as
Netherlorn. More recent, Census-derived designations refer to
roughly this same sub-area as Mid-Argyll. It is in this place in the
West Highlands of Scotland that the village of Ford is located.

The village of Ford may not appear on some maps of Scotland,

24

but with or without the testimony of mapmakers, it is there at the head of Loch Awe, inland a few scant miles from the many-fingered coastline of Mid-Argyll. It is four miles from its nearest neigh-bouring village, Kilmartin, and only two miles from the site of Carnasserie Castle, the home of Bishop Carswell, who in the 1600s translated the first book (Knox's liturgy) from English to Gaelic. Twenty-five miles to the north lies Oban, which is considered by most to be the 'capital city' of the West Highlands today. (It is a very long twenty-five miles, however, and the twisting, narrow, steep roadway discourages frequent shopping or business trips.) Oban is a busy, growing trade and tourist centre which influences not only a wide area of the mainland, but, through its extensive ferry service, is also linked to many of the western islands as well. While newspaper readers in Ford look at *The Scotsman* (Edinburgh) or the *Glasgow Herald* (or in a few instances *The Times*) for national and international news, they subscribe to the *Oban Times* and the *Argyllshire Advertiser* for regional coverage.

Twelve miles to the south is the growing town of Lochgilphead, situated on Loch Fyne just at the point where the Kintyre Peninsula begins. Lochgilphead is close enough to Ford (approximately twenty minutes) to be used as a shopping centre and place of work for many. It is changing rapidly from a sleepy village on the route from Inverary to Campbeltown and Oban to a district govern-mental centre, influenced by the reorganization of Scottish local authorities which took place in the 1970s. In a later chapter, we shall explore some of the ways in which growth and change in Lochgilphead influence the life of Ford.

From what is now the main road between Lochgilphead and Oban, a pleasant country road branches off to the east near Kilmartin to take the visitor the short distance of two and one-half miles to the village of Ford. The visual aspect is striking. The first impression is of ancient, rumpled green-velvet rugs thrown over lumpy hills. Whatever this section of the West Highlands lacks, in height, vastness, and the sense of endlessness which impresses the viewer in some other parts of the Highlands, is compensated for by this ancient velvet-rugged majesty. It feels close, warm, friendly, protecting, and at the same time, mysterious and curiosity-provoking: What made this place? Who has lived here? Sheep and cattle can be seen ruminating in the narrow valley and on the hillsides; their grazing is hampered by extensive growths of bracken and heather. There are almost no trees to be seen on this stretch of the road. There is an occasional house within sight of the road. We are not yet at the village itself, but we are within its pull, within its definition.

The old green hills through which we pass on this level, winding road show clearly the work of glaciers and of the sculpting effects of Loch Awe as it once went to the sea, for we are following the course of an unremembered river 'upstream' on this route to the village. The southern head of Loch Awe was once its foot, and its water rushed from north to south outward through the Kilmartin valley to the sea. Some great geological event changed the course of flow aeons ago so that the waters of Loch Awe now rush northward past the massive slopes of Ben Cruachan and through the Pass of Brander to Loch Etive, thence to the Firth of Lorn and the sea.

The occasional rock faces and crags reveal a limestone base underlying the thin, stony hillside soil. The barrenness of these contoured hills is attributable mainly to glaciation, thin topsoil, and the wetness of earlier climes which drowned the forests and created large areas of peat and boggy muck. (Evidence of heavy afforestation in an earlier epoch can be found in the perfectly preserved treestumps found buried in the peat in the Highlands where they have lain for thousands of years.) It is quiet here in the little water-worn passage from Kilmartin to the head of Loch Awe—quiet, green, and craggy. There is little or no traffic. There are signs of humanity past and present, but their activity and their leavings do not dominate the scene. The hills seem to be waiting. It is just a little eerie. This is *not* just another place.

Continuing up the road, past Eurach Farm on the right and Creaganterve Farm on the left, past the turn-off to Stroneskir Farm and the Kilmichael Glen to the south, Loch Ederline comes into view on the right, its sparkling water reaching almost to the edge of the road. Overlooking it on the hillside to the left of the road is Auchinellan Estate. The loch itself is the visitor's introduction to Ederline Estate, which extends south and east to include around thirteen thousand acres. A tiny river connects Loch Ederline with Loch Awe. It is at the ford of this river, a ford used by cattle-drovers and horse-drawn coaches until sometime in the nineteenth century, that the village of Ford is situated, and from which its name derives.

The 71 dwellings in Ford are complemented by a church, a grocery shop, a craft shop, a garage, and a village hall. Visually the village is dominated by the Ford Hotel. The community stretches out mainly on a line formed by the road which proceeds up the northwest side of Loch Awe through Dalavich to Taynuilt, and on a second line formed by the intersecting road which crosses over the little river opposite the hotel and continues to Cladich and Dalmally. The hotel is not the geographic or the population centre of the village, but, largely because of its pub life, it is the social and psychological centre of Ford.

Before describing the village further, a word about Loch Awe is in order. Loch Awe is a fresh-water loch, narrow in width and about twenty-three miles in length, lying on a southwest-to-northeast line paralleling Loch Linnhe and Loch Fyne. It may have taken its name from the Gaelic word *abh*, meaning 'river'. At the northern end of Loch Awe, under the huge shoulder of Ben Cruachan, lie the ruins of Kilchurn Castle, for centuries the stronghold of the Campbell clan before the seat of the Argyll power was moved to Inverary. King Robert the Bruce is said to have stayed here in the late thirteenth or early fourteenth century. It is now one of the most photographed castle ruins in Scotland, though the photographs are sometimes marred by the huge pylons and cables transporting hydroelectric power from the Falls of Cruachan power station. Centuries-old maps show this castle as well as other historic sites around the loch. There was once a convent on a tiny island in Loch Awe. The village of Cladich is noted by quite early travellers through the Highlands. The ruins of Ardchonnel Castle, near Eredine, can still be seen on an island scarcely larger than the castle's perimeter. Port Sonochan ('port of peace') can be found on some very early maps. The ruins of Finchairn Castle may be found near the southern end of Loch Awe adjacent to Finchairn Farm, which has been a part of Ederline Estate for hundreds of years. (The story is told that in the thirteenth century, in pre-Campbell days, this castle was destroyed by fire at the hands of an angry bridegroom who wished to prevent the laird from exercising his 'rights' with the vassal's bride on their wedding night.)

The Campbells held the entirety of Loch Awe at one time, and in fact their rise to prominence had its origin centuries ago when they were the 'Knights of Lochow'. Later, however, much of the southern two-thirds of Loch Awe was owned by the Malcolms of Poltalloch, who began to amass significant holdings in Mid-Argyll in the sixteenth century.

Historical records from the thirteenth through the seventeenth centuries contain the names of estates (almost always held by the Campbells) which are still in existence around the loch today as the names of farms, estates, residences, or government-owned forests: Finchairn, Ederline, Auchinellan, Glennan, Eredine, Inverliever, Stroneskir, Creaganterve, Braevallich—all these names have persevered around the southern end of Loch Awe for at least four hundred years, and some have been there for more than seven hundred years. A Vatican manuscript dated 6 March 1422 contains a reference to Kilineuair church, the roofless ruin of which still stands adjacent to the old drove road near Ford which leads to Auchendrain, near Inverary on Loch Fyne.[2] A charter from Alexander II dated 1 August 1240, said to be the oldest writ in existence dealing with lands in Argyll, refers to 'Fyncharne' and 'Glennane', among other lands.[3]

The history of human communities around Loch Awe is even more ancient than the written record or the crumbling walls of Kilineuair church, Kilchurn, Finchairn, and Carnassarie castles suggest. The whole area is rich with archaeological treasures dating back thousands of years to Pictish times, before the sons of Erc came from Ireland to Argyll eventually to found the Kingdom of Dalriada and plant the seeds of the Scottish nation. Standing stones remain as mute, ghostly guardians over many fields; stone kists or burial places still honour the dead in many places after the passage of fifty centuries. And the remains of creannogs, man-made islands of stone whereon tiny houses and byres were maintained in times of fear of marauding neighbours, the tops of these incredible rock piles can still be seen above the water when the level of the loch is sufficiently low. Cup-and-ring marks appear on many large stones in the area, clearly man-made but their meanings unknown. And atop the hills around Ford can be found evidence of forts of this same ancient age (hence the name of Dun Dubh, 'black fort', the highest hill at the southern end of the loch, rising near to the village of Ford). The stones endure from centuries before the birth of Christ. Loch Awe is more than just a geographic site, although that would be enough to make it interesting, given its grandeur and clear water. It is also a time linked to other times going back almost as far as the mind can imagine. A sense of time past lives with the people of places such as Ford today, although perhaps with less immediacy than with earlier generations, before television and highways crowded out the oral tradition.

Like the heavily-indented coastline and the sea and land-lochs of the whole of Argyll, Loch Awe was and is still an obstacle to north-south travel through Mid-Argyll. Before the second half of the nineteenth century, Loch Awe was something to be got around or got over for travellers from the south or cattle-drovers from Mull or Oban in North Lorn requiring access to central Scottish markets. Roads evolved along both the northern and southern tips of Loch Awe. There are records of travellers from Dalmally to Taynuilt in the eighteenth century (John Knox was among the more notable of this era), and wood and charcoal were brought southward to Loch Fyneside this way during that century. The road (probably merely a track) past the southern end, as well as crossings at Taychreggan, Sonochan, and similar sites, were developing around the same time. There was considerable traffic via steamers along the length of the Loch for many years beginning in the late nineteenth century, but travellers generally have depended on the north-south roads skirting Loch Awe's extremities to get them into or out of the West Highlands.

It was the road fording the small stream between Loch Ederline and Loch Awe which was used by these travellers to get around the southwest end of the Loch. It is this road, no longer used, which explains the presence of the village of Ford on this site today.

Ford included 59 occupied dwellings (excluding holiday residences) and 156 people as of November 1981. Clustered around the 'central' area of the village are the Ford Hotel, the Post Office and Telegraph, the Ford Church of Scotland, the grocery shop, the Craft Shop, and a mechanic's garage. Several detached family dwellings are located in this nuclear portion of the village, some quite old and some very new. In addition, there are four Council-built flats and six Forestry Commission flats built in 'rowhouse' fashion near the central part of the village.

While the central village could never be termed 'bustling', it is the area where the lives of the people of Ford intersect most frequently. Not only is Murray's pub at the Ford Hotel a magnet which draws people together, villagers also encounter each other frequently at the Post Office, where Maimie Cameron, the Postmistress, is ready with a cheerful word or a bit of news, or at Betty McLean's grocery shop across the road. Many will stop to chat with Mrs Ross, or her daughter Heather, or Lana McCuig at the Craft Shop, especially if they are waiting for the twice-weekly bus to Lochgilphead which turns around in the lane next to the shop. Because of their location, geographic and social, at the centre of things, few events could transpire in the village without the knowledge of David Murray, Maimie Cameron, Mrs Ross, and Betty McLean.

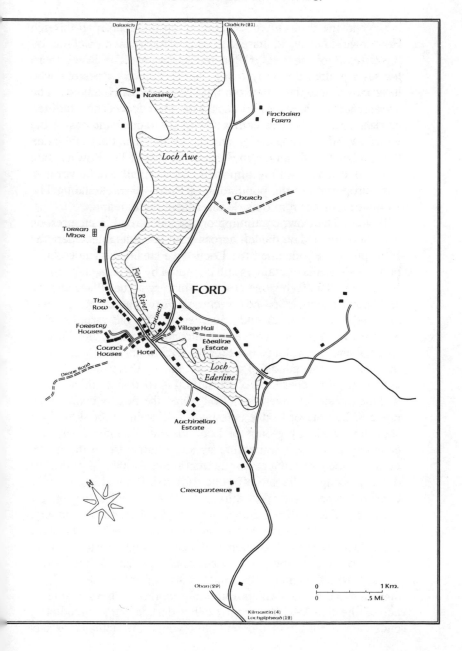

Beyond the Post Office, continuing up the main road through Ford toward Dalavich, there is a string of mostly new dwellings on the left side of the road. Often referred to as 'The Row', these houses are almost entirely owned and occupied by persons who have moved into the area from outside the West Highlands. The appearance of these new homes with their fenced and tailored gardens and yards is in contrast with the older buildings of the village. While housing design and materials are not a useful index to the origins of all families in Ford, in the case of The Row it is safe to say that almost all are imported. As we shall see, however, a large proportion of the population of Ford—even excluding The Row—originated from outside the Mid-Argyll area.

Beyond The Row, continuing on the same road, a picturesque cottage is situated on the left across from the quiet inlet where the Ford pier once welcomed the Loch Awe steamers. The cottage, built by a steamer captain, is still occupied by his daughter-in-law. It is a reminder of a bygone era in the history of the village and the loch. Some distance beyond this cottage lie two more small clusters of dwellings at Torran and Inverliever. The old farmhouse at Torran Mor has been converted into eight flats by the District Council and a new house built for the McKinnons, who now farm the land. In the minds of some people in the village, Torran constitutes the upper limit of Ford on this road, but others would include the site of Inverliever Lodge and the nearby commercial nursery. Inverliever Lodge is today a retreat-like school used for short-term visits by groups of London school children, who are encouraged to learn something about country life in the north, thanks to the terms of a generous trust set up for this purpose. The nursery occupies the site of a one-time fish farm. It is a thriving concern owned by a Yorkshire man. Two families live on the premises. The road continues past the Lodge and the nursery, passing through heavily planted forest groves on the hills above the lochside on its way to Dalavich, and then on eventually to Taynuilt.

If we retrace our route to the central village and take the road to Cladich which intersects the main road in front of the hotel, we cross a small bridge (which ultimately replaced the original fords across the 'black water' from Loch Ederline) and immediately encounter a cluster of old buildings which are actually part of

Ederline Estate. On the left is North Lodge, which looks across to the sagging gates which guard the original, but now unused, entrance to Ederline House. Beyond it are the smiddy and the school and schoolhouse, now used as private dwellings. On the right are the Village Hall and two recently-built bungalows. Past this cluster of buildings lies the present entrance to Ederline Estate, which contains not only the present manor house, but the original eighteenth century mansion house, several farm buildings, and the houses of some of the workers employed to operate the estate farm. Beyond Ederline is Finchairn Farm and the ruins of Kilineuair Church. The road continues another twenty miles to Cladich and Dalmally on the southeast lochside.

Knowledge of the setting of Ford is incomplete without some characterization of the local economy. And while the next chapter provides a more detailed description of the economic and social history of the area, it will be useful to paint some of this history in broad strokes here.

Farming has occupied many residents of the Ford area over the centuries. But the soil is not especially rich or deep; it is thin and rocky and acidic, and there is little level, rich earth which is dry or expansive enough to permit tillage on a basis required for a competitive agricultural market. The climate in this section of the West Highlands, with its annual average rainfall of over eighty inches, also works against successful crop-farming. The earth is often boggy even on steep slopes, and the constant rain and drizzle 'renders farming here very precarious, and often unprofitable', as an eighteenth century writer observed. For two centuries, farming in this area has meant hillside farming: the grazing of sheep and cattle. And despite the strong winds of economic change in rural Scotland, hillside farming continues as an important part of the economic base of Ford.

In the last seventy years, forestry has also become important to Ford as a source of employment as the Forestry Commission bought up estates and former sheep farms and planted thousands of acres of trees. Private landowners have also practised extensive afforestation. Private contractors together with the Forestry Commission provide numerous jobs in connection with site preparation, planting, vermin control, thinning, harvesting, and transportation.

Tourism also provides employment for a number of the villagers, mainly in the season from April to October. The Ford Hotel, operated by David Murray and his family, contains ten rooms with a total of twenty beds, a dining room and a pub, with boat facilities for guests who come for the fishing. In addition to the three members of the family and a kitchen helper/cleaner who are busy year-round with running the hotel and bar, a full-time and a part-time cook, a receptionist, and a waitress/cleaner are hired during the summer months. In recent years two bed and breakfast facilities have been opened, providing additional seasonal income for the families involved. The services of a few of the men are available when visitors come for the shooting. Other villagers, as mentioned earlier, are employed in the Post Office, the grocery shop, the Craft Shop, and the nursery. One is a garage mechanic.

In every instance described so far, the work in which the people of Ford are involved is in the village itself or quite close by. A significant and increasing number of the residents of Ford work not only outside their homes and family businesses, but outside the village altogether. As we shall see in a subsequent chapter, most of the outside employment is in Lochgilphead, where people from Ford work as teachers, nurses, secretaries, and government employees, but at least one works in Oban and another has travelled as far as Egypt in his work as a geologist.

From this brief review of the means of livelihood among the people of Ford, it is obvious that the economic base is quite diverse. Ford is not a single-economy village tied solely, as some villages are, to fishing or to tourism or to employment in a single large factory, and certainly not to farming. Perhaps this diversity will surprise those who still think of the West Highlands villages as remote, self-sufficient agricultural outposts. The diversity in employment, and especially the presence of a 'commuting' workforce, are simply a reflection of the changes in political and economic systems which have joined previously remote areas into larger regional, national, and international networks, and which have bound small places into systems created by large ones. It is now possible, for example, for a geologist to choose to live in Ford, though his work takes him to the North Sea oil fields on the other side of the country or to Egyptian oil fields on the other side of the world, because in twenty minutes he can board the Lochgilphead helicopter shuttle to Glasgow.

Even the maintenance of traditional hill-farming is made possible because of policies determined in Brussels, where members of the European Economic Community assemble. Neither new nor old economic forms are unaffected by increasingly centralized and distant systems, and the connections between localities and centres of power which would have been unthinkable a few decades ago are strong, despite their distances. One can imagine that in other instances, such as the coalfields of Appalachia, the growth of these connections between localities and power centres leads to the 'assignment' of single economic functions, such as mineral extraction, to particular localities. In the Highlands of Scotland, Aviemore is such a place, specializing in tourism. But in the case of Ford, which may be an exception rather than the rule, economic diversity has increased, not declined.

On the other hand, lest it be concluded that there is in Ford a miniaturized reflection of the kind of occupational diversity one would find in the city, it should be emphasized that agriculture is still important—agriculture and the growing of trees, which easily account for most of the work in the Ford area. Even in summer, tourism is secondary in terms of providing work for people in Ford.

The nature of agricultural enterprises in and around Ford is worth describing at this point, because it is certainly not what it has been in the past and not what it would be like in other regions and countries. Coming into Ford, the eye is first drawn to the colours and shapes of the landforms. Then one notices the stock: the sheep and cattle. But it is obvious even to the uninformed foreigner that these are not 'farms' in the sense of smallholdings. They are estates. They have been estates for hundreds of years, and what they are today and how they are perceived is influenced by that history even if they are not operated in the ways they would have been in the past. As we shall come to see in more detail in the next chapter, these estates are owned by private landowners, although often not the same lairds who owned them years ago, because many of the estates have changed hands as the fortunes of families ebbed and flowed. We will also see how the functions of estates have changed from one historical era to another, and that farming for profit is only one such function.

When reference is made to a 'farmer' in the estate system, it is the landowner who is usually meant. The employees of the owner who perform the tasks of farming are the shepherds, the stockmen, the woodmen and foresters. (In fact, when the Scottish Census of Agriculture counts agricultural workers, the farmer and his wife are excluded from the enumeration.)

There are, however, farms which are not part of privately owned estates. One such farm is Torran, operated by Mr McKinnon. Farms such as Torran are owned by government agencies and leased to private individuals. The Forestry Commission owns some farms in Scotland, as does the Department of Ag.iculture. They are only for lease, not for sale. The estates are generally of very large size, and when they are available for sale they are well beyond the financial capabilities of potential smallholders. Because so much farmland is either Crown land or estate land, the idea of 'buying a farm' is a somewhat unusual one compared to a country like the United States.

Thus there are no smallholders in Ford. Nor are there any crofts around Ford. The remains of what are said locally to have been crofts are visible on the site of the original Glennan farm and at the foot of Dun Dubh. Although crofting existed throughout Argyll at one time, the pattern eroded earlier in this part of the West Highlands than farther to the north. In fact, there are no tenants of any kind on the farms around Ford except for those like Mr McKinnon, if by 'tenant' we mean a person who pays rent to occupy and use a farm, keeping the earnings from the farm for himself. The farmers working Ederline today, for example, are employees of the landowner and work the land and stock for him.

Farming is the most traditional of livelihoods in this area, although it is done with machinery and chemicals, with the latest technical advice from the West of Scotland Agricultural College, with crucial government subsidies, and with an eye on international market conditions and EEC agricultural policies. Although it is very close to the sea coast, no one in Ford is involved in fishing, and the time when men followed the herring fishing for part of the year, although it is recorded in documents about the parish, is not within memory. In terms of acreage, public investments, employment, value of products, forestry is the economic sector which has grown most rapidly in this century, influencing farming, housing, population composition, and the way of life of residents of Ford. The growth of forestry has meant the shrinkage of grazing land (at the approximate ratio of three acres per sheep, large quantities of grazing land are essential to support any significant hill farming operation), and as the number of men involved in forest planting increased, the number of shepherds and cattlemen has declined somewhat in this immediate vicinity.

The estates continue to be important to the locality, however, even if they are not the elaborate country palaces of the wealthy British elite which they once were, even if they do not involve the crofting or other varieties of tenantry which still survive in other parts of the Highlands and in the Western isles, and even if they do not employ directly as many people as they did earlier in this century. Their importance today lies in the fact that, together with the Crown, estates such as Ederline and Auchinellan still control the largest quantities of acreage available for agricultural purposes; what uses are made of these lands still today determines the livelihoods of many local families and thereby influences the economic bases of communities like Ford.

The coming of the Forestry Commission to Ford in 1907 is inseparable from the history of the estates of Poltalloch, Ederline, and Auchinellan. Simultaneously with this history flows the evolution of what would now be called 'tourism' in the area. All of these stories are important to understand as background to the origin and shaping of the village of Ford, and to the comings and goings of its people. A more detailed comprehension of the historical environment of Ford may help us understand how the fates of localities like it are strongly influenced by events, forces, and individuals distant from them. We turn now to an account of that historical setting.

Footnotes

[1] An excellent sketch of Argyll's history and the Campbell influence can be found in Eric Cregeen, 'The Changing Role of the House of Argyll in the Scottish Highlands', in N.T. Phillipson and Rosalind Mitchison (eds.), *Scotland in the Age of Improvement: Essays in Scottish History in the 18th Century* (Edinburgh: University Press, 1970), pp. 5-23.

[2] J.R.N. McPhail, ed., *Highland Papers*, Vol. IV (Edinburgh: University Press, 1934), pp. 177-8.

[3] J.R.N. McPhail, ed., *Highland Papers*, Vol. II (Edinburgh: University Press for the Scottish Historical Society, 1916), p. 121.

3 The Historical Setting

Meanwhile the Highlands may become the fairy ground for romance and poetry, or the subject of experiment for the professors of speculation, political and economical. But if the hour of need should come— and it may not, perhaps, be far distant—the pibroch may sound through the deserted region, but the summons will remain unanswered.
Sir Walter Scott
Tales of a Grandfather

The people of Ford today live side by side and on top of the history of others who have occupied the area they now temporarily claim as theirs. It is a history both ancient and immediate. It covers an incredible span of time, but because of recent rapid change, 'history' is also felt as something that happened recently, as if time were nipping at one's heels. It is important to understand some of this history because it is a 'lived-with' history: the people of Ford carry it with them and experience it almost daily in one way or another. Their knowledge of it may not always be deep, but their awareness that it is there is inescapable. Elements of that history make up part of the lore of Ford, its place-names, the names of some of its current inhabitants, the names of people who have just passed away, the stories of the area and its places, the myths about where Ford and its people and places originated and, therefore, what they are like today and what will become of them in the future (their 'mythic charter').

Although, for example, only six persons living in Ford today speak Gaelic, there is not a person in the village who does not know that Gaelic was once the predominant tongue, if not the only one. Place-names such as Dun Dubh, Creaganterve, and Torranbeg are reminders of this inheritance. Recent incomers for the most part share this knowledge and an appreciation for it, often giving their new bungalows Gaelic-based names from the area. Even some of the village pets carry this reminder of the linguistic inheritance, carrying Gaelic names such as Duishge, 'black water', after the name of a stretch of river water across from the Ford Hotel.

Although few villagers belong to the local historical society, almost all will respond to the question 'What is Ford like?' by first establishing that its area is important in history, and everyone is a walking catalogue of local landmarks, ruins, old roads, and ancient monuments. Perhaps it is not surprising that the people of Ford are so conscious of history; it may only be remarkable to one who comes from a people who have so little history of which to have a sense. But it would be difficult to imagine ignoring the daily reminders of the past with which this place is so generously furnished: standing stones, burial kists, cairns, hill forts, croft ruins, demolished mansions, decaying piers, the incredibly ancient and glaciated hills with their more recent, possibly fourteen-hundred-year-old names. These objects speak in silent voices to the people of Ford, and the communion of the people with them over many generations has made them a part of the living present. The past, or what the people think and know about it, contributes strongly to the sense of place held by the residents of Ford, old and new, and it is therefore important to learn what that past has been like.

Obviously, it is also important to know the past for the trite but convincing reason that professional historians give when they justify their pastimes to us: it is difficult to understand the present without knowing from where it came. Where the reader's familiarity with the history of estate systems, population movements, hill farming, forestry, and sport and tourism in the West Highlands can be assumed, the amount of space I will give in this section to the past may seem excessive. But the truth is that few people outside Scotland have much comprehension of the social and economic history of this area. Some attention to what life has been like in the Mid-Argyll of earlier times should therefore be helpful to those who want to know what it is like today. The points of continuity between past and present should be illuminating; the points of departure should be more easily highlighted.

Early History

The archaeological evidence of human communities in the area of which Ford is a part stretches as far back as 4000-5000 years.[1] From the Mesolithic Age (which is not the first age to have seen humans in occupancy here, merely one from which there are numerous leavings), the Mid-Argyll area has inherited a large number of easily-seen stone burial cairns, many of them chambered. Several of these imposing and eerie rockpiles can be seen along the Kilmartin valley, almost in a line, following the old river bed which once took melted glacier water to the sea. Most of the mounds have been entered by succeeding generations of local residents and farmers, amateur explorers, and trained archaeologists, and some may have been used for burial by inhabitants from more than one era. The stone kist which lies next to the bridge in Ford across from the hotel goes by the Gaelic name of *Cnoc an Ath* ('hillock of the ford'); it is so covered in vegetation that it is not recognizable for what it is except by the people who live there. Apparently *Cnoc an Ath* has never been excavated, and while everyone in Ford knows about it, they respectfully leave it alone. One can easily imagine that the bones of the Stone Age dead lie there yet next to the bridge, watching the site of the old ford, shrouded by earth, moss, and a lush growth of rhododendron.

In Scotland, and especially in Argyll, stones are the ubiquitous bearers of messages from every layer of time. Standing stones populate the entire countryside—in Ford there is one in a field next to the hotel, and another at the original site of Glennan Farm, and another at the back of Mr MacKinnon's new farmhouse (that one with a cross carved on it, possibly from a later era). These erect slabs stand six to eight feet above the ground and are countersunk another four feet or so. There is a complete circle of them near Kilmartin surrounding a burial cairn, and there are other sets of them standing in fields nearby. Most are unmarked, or if they once bore markings, they have disappeared with the years, and we are left with only guesses about their significance, which, like that of Stonehenge, may have been religious.

There are other stones from this and more recent eras. Some are dimpled with man-made 'cup and ring' marks of unknown meaning.

One of these stones is embedded in the earth on the verge of Mr MacKinnon's field at Torran Mor. Stone forts of various generations are still to be seen atop many crags in the area including Ford, where one stares down from a hill near the road at Torran Mor and another watches over the drove road and the village from atop Creag a'Chapuill. And there are crannogs, the curious, tiny, man-made islands of stone barely large enough for a family's black house and byre, which can be seen when the water is low in both Loch Ederline and Loch Awe near Ford, stirring the imagination with stories of desperate times long ago when these defenses must have been needed to protect families and their stock from the raids of neighbours.

Human communities were here ages before there were Scots, and even long before there were Picts—and we know little even about those folk. Romans, Normans, Picts, Celts, Scots and Norse have all been here trampling the remains of earlier folk, perhaps wondering at the meanings of these legacies of stone just as we do today. Occasionally, remains other than those of stone are unearthed, as in the case of the exciting find in which Sheena Carmichael's late husband, Alasdair, was involved, and which is named the Torran Hoard. Accompanied by his young son, and amateur archaeologist Marion Campbell, Alasdair discovered, lying on the ground near a rock cliff in his back yard at Torranbeg, an unusually well-preserved collection of axe heads and bracelets from the Bronze Age. It must have been a time of excitement not only for the Carmichaels but for all of Ford. The items are on display today in the Museum of Antiquities in Edinburgh.

One of the most significant sites—probably *the* most important from the standpoint of history—is the hill fort of Dunadd lying just beyond Kilmartin from Ford. Dating from the close of the fifth century AD, the hill of Dunadd (or 'the fort on the Add River') was the capital of Dalriada, the ancient kingdom of Scotland formed when the three sons of Erc are said to have invaded Argyll successfully from the Antrim coast of Ireland. The hill rises like a small surprise from the old sea floor, (now the boggy Crinan Moss), and it dominates the view when one drives today from Lochgilphead to Kilmartin. On top of the hill, among the ruins, can still be seen the coronation stone with a footprint clearly visible on the surface toward one end and the figure of a wild boar carved on its flank. A ceremonial bowl is carved into another nearby stone. It was to Dunadd that the Stone of Destiny, Jacob's Pillow, was said to have been brought from Ireland—the stone which was later moved to Scone and then to Westminster. This is the site where Scotland's kings were crowned for many generations. This looming lump of rock in Argyll can rightly be called the cradle of the Scottish nation.

From this site, beginning with the sixth century and continuing into the early middle ages, efforts were directed by the Scottish kings to subdue the Picts, establish peace among conflicting factions, and consolidate a kingdom. In later years as what became the Highland clan system was evolving, the area witnessed inter-familial warfare and depredation. Scotland's kings, and later England's would continue to bring order and unity and peace to the entire region through force of superior arms. Loyal service in those wars of pacification would be rewarded with charters, writs, and grants of large tracts of land. Powerful landowners, kinsmen of or loyal supporters of royalty, made their homes in fortified houses and castles, most of which lie in ruins today, but a few of which, like Duntrune Castle on Loch Crinan, are still inhabited.

Argyll, largely because of the powerful role of the Campbell clan, that large, complex, and forceful collection of families which always seemed to show a knack for backing the winning side, was brought under centralized control considerably earlier than the rest of the Highlands. In recognition of their loyalty and indispensable service to various crowns, beginning, apparently, in the thirteenth century with a grant from Robert the Bruce, the Campbells were given control of most of Argyll, of which eventually they were made earls, and later, dukes. Clan ownership evolved gradually into private ownership (again earlier in Argyll than in other parts of the Highlands[2]) but generations of the same families—almost inevitably Campbells—managed to keep title to their lands for what now seem incredible lengths of time, usually hundreds of years. The system of estates and farms which exists today developed in this context.

Brief historical sketches of the three estates which have played prominent roles in the background of Ford will provide an appropriate introduction to the history of the village itself. None of these histories is finished, of course—the scenes of the continuing drama are playing yet today. With the main elements of the historical background in hand, it should become easier to comprehend the significance of recent change and current forces at work in Ford today.

Poltalloch

One of the major estates which has played a strongly influential role in the history of Ford is Poltalloch. Weighed against the influence of Ederline and Auchinellan, Poltalloch's part in this history has in fact been by far the strongest, even, indirectly, in this century; at one time it owned almost the entire area around Ford with the exception of Ederline and Auchinellan.

Until 1907, Poltalloch Estate encompassed most of the north side of Loch Awe, down to and including significant parts of Ford village itself. (The dividing line between former Poltalloch and Auchinellan lands would have lain somewhere between the present Ford Hotel, which was once the Auchinellan Inn, and the present Clough house, once known as the Crown House and earlier called the Change-house, referred to in the Valuation Rolls from the mid- to late-1800s as 'Ford Inn'. The lands along Loch Awe formed only a portion of the more than 82,000 acres owned by Poltalloch in the nineteenth century when the estate enjoyed its grandest days.[3]

The connection between Ford and Poltalloch Estate today is not so direct as in those earlier times. The long-time residents of the village today know about the estate; they are acquainted with some of its history and its present laird. Sheena Carmichael was born at Slockavullin on the estate, five miles from where she lives in Ford today on land once owned by Poltalloch, and her father was a butler in Poltalloch House. But what happens at Poltalloch now has no important and direct consequences for Ford. The relationship is that of neighbour to neighbour, though the neighbours may belong to different class levels.

It was not always thus. The Malcolms of Poltalloch were more than neighbours before 1907; they owned much of Ford and the

lochside, having somehow acquired these lands from the Campbells and others over the centuries, beginning with the first
Malcolm, Donald McGillespie VicOlchallum of Poltalloch (c.
1530-1609), first laird.[4] In the seventeenth, eighteenth and nineteenth centuries, the Malcolms of Poltalloch, the Campbells of
Ederline, and the Campbells and successive owners of Auchinellan
exercised controlling interest in the little village which lay on the
intersecting boundaries of the three estates (as well as on the
boundary between two church and civil parishes). But it is likely
that because the Malcolms owned more land in and around Ford,
theirs was the more important influence on its affairs and its fate.[5]

An example of this influence can be seen in the history of the
Ford Church of Scotland. Although the church is now the shared
responsibility of the two parishes of Glassary and Kilmartin,
historically it was attached to the Kilmartin church (in the heart of
Malcolm country). The Kirk Session minutes dating back to the
late 1600s include the names of many people in the Ford area—
both as communicants and miscreants.[6] So it must have been only
natural that when the Presbytery of Inverary set up a committee to
establish a separate church at Ford, it was organized out of the
Kilmartin church with its minister, Reverend Donald Jackson, as
chairman. The Revd Jackson's report to Presbytery in 1853
reveals that the land upon which the church was built four years
earlier belonged to Poltalloch, and was leased to the church for one
shilling per year. (The laird also made a generous contribution of
£50 towards the building of the church, larger than any but the gift
of £180 from the Committee for Church Extension in the Highlands.) The Ford Church of Scotland held its first Divine Service in
October, 1850, with the obvious blessing of the laird. The church at
Kilmartin has always been associated with Poltalloch—the ancient
Poltalloch gravestones are among its priceless possessions. The
church at Ford was not only associated with the great estate but,
according to the record, was made possible by it.

Not only was the church land part of Poltalloch, but so was the
Change-house, the land where the post office and telegraph were
established sometime in the late nineteenth century, the gravel
quarry, the site of the present Forestry houses and Council houses
next to the old drove road, and all the farmland from Salachry and

Dun Dubh northeastward up the lochside to and including Barmaddy. On the south lochside, Braevallich was part of Poltalloch, as was Glennan located across from Creaganterve east of the village.

When the Crinan Canal was created almost two hundred years ago, the laird of Poltalloch gave serious thought to building an extension from Loch Awe to the Crinan. The Crinan canal itself made it possible for vessels from the Western Isles to sail in safe water directly to the Clyde, avoiding the long trip through the open sea around Kintyre. Writing in the late eighteenth century, one observer expressed his view that the canal would bring two important commodities from the south to Mid-Argyll to improve life there: coal and salt.[7] Had another canal been created from Loch Awe to the Crinan, it would have made traffic possible between the Clyde, Loch Linnhe, Fort William, Orchy, Dalmally, the Western Isles, and even eventually to Perth, with Poltalloch at the connecting point in the middle. Ford would have been directly on the route, placed as it is at the head of Loch Awe, and it is difficult to imagine what effect this decision would have had in transforming the village. Although plans for the additional canal were drawn up, the project was later abandoned.[8]

Likewise, Ford would have been rather drastically influenced by the building of a railroad for which plans were once laid at the request of Poltalloch. The proposed Ardrishaig and Loch Awe Railway was, one supposes, intended to make possible the same commercial routes the earlier canal scheme had envisioned.[9] But this plan, too, was set aside, and Ford was not to experience the effects of either Poltalloch scheme. Thus, decisions made at Poltalloch Estate often had consequences for Ford. And it was inevitable that what happened to the fortunes of Poltalloch would have an influence on the future of Ford, marginal though the little village was to the interests of the great estate.

Just before the turn of this century, several events took place upon which the future of Poltalloch seems to have turned. John Malcolm, one of the more successful and colourful lairds, died in the eighteen-nineties, leaving death duties to be borne by his son, John Wingfield Malcolm, who in turn died in 1902, leaving whatever problems he had inherited to his next oldest brother,

Edward Donald Malcolm, the present laird's great-grandfather. But the death duties were not the most important problem inherited by this laird. Death duty laws of any consequence were not put into effect until 1910 under Lloyd George, and even then there were major loopholes which permitted large gifts tax-free, provided they were given seven years before the death of the donor, until these loopholes were closed in 1974. A more important factor in the fate of the estate around the turn of the century was the failure of the family sugar plantations in Jamaica. The Malcolms had held significant interests in those plantations for well over one hundred years, and in fact the well-being of Poltalloch Estate had probably become dependent on the vast profits made from sugar for much of the nineteenth century. When sugar failed, a reassessment of the future of Poltalloch was required, since it had not paid its own way for years.

Situations like this were, in fact, not unusual among Scottish estates in the late nineteenth and early twentieth centuries, though the timing of the reckoning varied considerably, and some probably have not even now reached the point yet where they require economic self-sufficiency. According to historian Roy Campbell, most of these estates were entirely dependent upon the infusion of money made elsewhere—in lowland Scotland, in England, or outside Britain altogether—from around 1870 to the nineteen-thirties. (In fact, it is the fairly widely accepted view of scholars that Scottish estates did not earn income for their owners but instead cost them rather dearly. The owner's profits were not usually made on the backs of the Scottish peasants who worked their estates, but on the backs of the English working class, or those of slaves and peasants elsewhere. These profits made elsewhere were turned into the equivalent of subsidies to maintain large estates in the north. The motives of the owners may well be questioned, if it is true that their interest in the estates was not profit. The answer lies in the prestige they enjoyed and still often enjoy among their peers, and the pleasure they took and still often take in the sport and recreation they can afford for themselves and invited friends.)

At the turn of the century Poltalloch was losing money, as it might well have been doing for some time, but now apparently there was no wealth from Jamaican sugar to meet the obligations—cash was required from some other source, and the largest asset held by the estate was land. At a time when it was most necessary, the family was unable to economize. Poltalloch House became a millstone. Business acumen, for which the family had been noted earlier, appeared to wane. Moreover, this set of circumstances, in the view of the current laird, Robin Malcolm, is probably what led to the sale of a number of farmlands around Loch Awe in 1907.

The sale is recorded in a deed dated November 1907. The deed records the fact that for £25,000, the Crown, in the form of the Commissioners of His Majesty's Woods, Forests, and Land Revenues, bought numerous parcels of Poltalloch land on Loch Awe from a trust which had been set up in 1903 consisting of Edward Donald Malcolm and three others. Those parcels closest to Ford included the farms, lands, and fishings of Inverlievermore, Inverlieverbeg, Kilmaha, Arichamish, Torran Mor, Torranbeg, and Salachry. The portions of Ford village which belonged to the estate were sold to the government as part of this transaction. Ford is in fact referred to as part of Torranbeg farm:

> . . . also All and Whole the lands of Torranbeg comprehending Upper Torranbeg and Lower Torranbeg with the pendicle thereof called Ford and with houses biggings parts pendicles privileges and pertinents thereof lying in the Barony of Lochow [Loch Awe] and Sheriffdom of Argyll . . .[10]

This sale of part of the estate to the Crown had a major influence on the future of the Ford area, because it opened the way for forestry, at first public, but later both public and private, which dominated the economy for many years. The door to forestry was opened because of the shrinkage of Poltalloch, and thus without stretching the truth we can conclude that the area around Ford was transformed from predominantly hillfarming to forestry in the early part of the twentieth century because of the failure of sugar in Jamaica.

Poltalloch Estate continued to shrink as the century progressed. The diminution of the estate can be attributed to a combination of factors: the continued absence of infusions of money from outside sources, the failure of attempts to make the estate itself profitable or self-sufficient, the enjoyment of high living (and spending) by successive incumbents in the lairdship, the imposition of increasingly high tax rates on estate property, the closing of loopholes in death duty legislation, and, most important in the last ten to fifteen years, the escalation of debt service costs as interest rates have climbed.

A major sale of property occurred in 1954 under the direction of the present laird's father, Lt.-Col. G.I. Malcolm. The prospectus prepared for this sale announces that the major portion of Poltalloch, 'the Noted Residential, Agricultural, and Sporting Estate', is to be auctioned in September.[11] The brochure describes the extent and magnificence of the estate and its buildings; exaggeration and flowery language were unnecessary because the size and magnificence of the place were self-evident. A total of 3,566 acres were to be sold. Numerous houses, cottages, and buildings were also for sale, including the majestic Poltalloch House, built in the Victorian era (1860) which contained 'five handsome principal apartments, fifteen bed and dressing rooms, six bathrooms—the remainder arranged as seven modern flats.' The mansion boasted a clock tower, a pipe organ, and a balcony for a piper. Schools, shops, churches (including the Poltalloch Church of England chapel built by the Malcolms themselves), would be convenient to prospective purchasers, and the estate was 'just under three and one-half hours by motor from Glasgow', according to the brochure.

Much of the land was sold at this auction, but Poltalloch House, which by now had become a millstone, was not. (Robin Malcolm tells that a prospective purchaser from America showed strong interest in the mansion house, but that, unfortunately, he died at Prestwick Airport on his way home.) At that time, any building with a roof, whether occupied or not, was subject to property taxes. Unable to maintain the high taxes levied on the monstrous old house, the Malcolms contracted with a demolition firm to sell what could be sold from it and then remove the roof. The demolition took place in 1960, one hundred years after the house was built. The ruins are there to be seen today.

The Malcolms, meanwhile, had modernized Duntrune Castle, which dates from the Norman era in the thirteenth century,[12] and moved into it. Important both architecturally and historically, Duntrune Castle is the home of the current generation of Malcolms. While Robin Malcolm enjoys his shooting, the castle, and the fine sunsets he can see across the waters of Loch Crinan from his study, he spends most of his time supervising the farming which takes place on the estate, devoting himself earnestly to turning the remaining 5,000 acres of Poltalloch into a productive and profitable farm. He is also an elected member of the District Council, and is active in the National Farmers' Union of Scotland and related agricultural organizations. In contrast with the dozens of families who once resided on the estate and were employed full-time as farmers, gamekeepers, woodmen and foresters, and house servants, five men are now employed full-time and one part-time on the estate. It would not be uncommon today to see Mr Malcolm out in the fields seeing to the 1,600 sheep or 300 cows, or overseeing the running of the combine, or trimming tree limbs along the long, single-track road that takes one on the grand sweep to the castle.

The Malcolms are determined to keep the lands and the castle intact, even if it requires selling off some of the priceless antiques which have furnished the homes of the Poltalloch lairds for centuries. Their biggest obstacle is the same enemy facing many such estates today: debt service resulting from loans negotiated years ago when they were prudent, before inflation and staggering interest rates began to test the whole estate system.[13]

Ederline

Ederline Estate today comprises about thirteen thousand acres. It may have been larger in earlier times, although not much larger, and never near the size of Poltalloch Estate. Like Poltalloch and virtually every other estate in Scotland, however, Ederline has experienced fundamental changes in its function and purposes. These changes have not been without consequences for Ford, of which it is a part. Among the more important of those changes has been its ownership.

The earliest maps of Scotland (or at least those which show that the mapmakers possessed any knowledge of the place) are those by Abraham Ortelius (1573), Gerard Mercator (1595), and Willem and Johan Blaeu (1635).[14] The Ortelius map shows a symbol resembling a castle at the head of Loch Awe, near where Ford would be today, with the name 'Eÿl' next to it. The Mercator and Blaeu maps give the same identification, perhaps following Ortelius, except that it is 'Eyl' without the umlaut. Was there a castle there in the early Middle Ages, and could it have been Norse in origin? By 1654, with the Robert Gordon map, numerous place-names appear up and down the loch, and there at the head, where it should appear, is 'Edder Lin'.

But there is a much earlier reference to 'Edyrling' which suggests that the estate had been in existence for 300 years before the seventeenth century. This reference appears in a set of early papers dealing with Glassary, collected in Volume II of *Highland Papers* by J.R.N. McPhail.[15] In this collection, there is a document describing a charter 'by David II to Gilbert of Glacestr of the lands of Edyrling and others, May 5, 1346'. (An even earlier charter, said to be the oldest writ in existence relating to lands in Argyll, shows Alexander II giving 'Funcharne' and 'Glennane' to one Gillascop MacGilchrist, dated August 1, 1240.[16] Finchairn adjoins Ederline Estate and has usually been included with the lands there historically, so the record of this portion of Ederline can be said to stretch back over 700 years.)

Another reference to 'Edderling' appears in 1620 in 'The Argyll Sasines', a collection of legal documents pertaining to properties in Argyllshire beginning in the early seventeenth century. It is interesting not only because it established a date and ownership by part of the Campbell family, but because it shows how families built their fortunes through prudent marriage arrangements:[17]

> 31 March 1620. Sasine of the liferent of the four merk land of Over Fincharne, 3 merk land of Edderling beg . . . given by Mr. Niall Campbell of Edderling, rector of Glassary, to his wife Jean, . . . in implement of their antenuptial marriage contract, dated at Glasgow, 11 and 28 February and 6 March 1620.

Ederline appears to have changed hands more than once during the seventeenth century, and then in 1662 it seems to have settled in the hands of one Colin Campbell of Blythswood.

The Campbell lineage is confusing for all who have spent less than a lifetime attempting to untangle it, but all of them are related in one way or another to the ancient progenitor, Ian Campbell, who assisted Robert the Bruce in defeating the MacDougalds at the

Pass of Brander in 1308 and who was, for his support and loyalty, given the MacDougald lands, thus launching the Campbell rise to power in Argyll which ultimately led to dukedom. Kilchurn Castle was built by a Sir Colin Campbell, Lord of Lochow, near the Pass of Brander in the fifteenth century (he died in 1480 at the age of 80).[18] Another Colin Campbell (Cailein Mor, or 'Big Colin') had been killed by MacDougalds around 1294—he was also known as a Knight of Lochow.[19] 'Colin' remained a popular name among Campbells, as the name appears in legal documents in 1662 in connection with Ederline and again in 1720 in the same connection.[20] Two more Colin Campbells of Ederline appear in the later eighteenth and early nineteenth centuries—the last, Major Colin Campbell, died in 1824.[21] Whether and how these Colin Campbells were related to 'Caelein Mor' or to the Earls and Dukes of Argyll, I do not know, but we can be sure that they were related in some fashion: they were definitely part of the famous Campbell dynasty.

Ederline remained in Campbell hands until around 1870, according to the present owner and what can be inferred from the record. In 1844, William Campbell of Ederline is mentioned in the *New Statistical Account of Scotland*.[22] When the Valuation Rolls begin in 1855-56, Ederline is in the possession of 'the heirs of William Campbell'; and then by 1860-61 it passes to Alexander Duncan Campbell, who still holds it in 1865-66.[23] Then by 1872-73, the ownership has changed to the Bruces of Elgin, when 'Henry Bruce of Ederline' appears to have taken advantage of some reversal in the fortunes of the Campbells of Ederline.[24] The Campbell chain was broken, at least at Ederline, by that year.

Henry Bruce's interest in Ederline Estate, like that of many new purchasers of Scottish estates at this time, was in sport, not agriculture, according to the present owner. Ederline was transformed from a farm into a recreational site, albeit on a grand scale, mirroring what was happening at other estates such as those in nearby Morvern.[25] In developing Ederline into the first-rate shooting and fishing estate and the holiday home for the family that it was to become, Henry Bruce was merely moving with the times, times which encompassed Ford as well as much of the rest of rural Scotland, especially the Highlands. This was the same era in which the steamers appeared in Loch Awe, transporting not only goods but holiday visitors as well, people of more than moderate means from the cities of Scotland and England who sought either the excellent fishing or the peace of Loch Awe, or both. What others could afford only for a week or two, or for a weekend, Henry Bruce could afford year-round, and when he was not in residence, he rented it to others, including its future owners, for sporting purposes.

The development or transformation of sporting estates followed naturally after the example set by Queen Victoria herself, whose well-known romance with Scotland's Highlands resulted in the construction in 1855 of Balmoral Castle, still used as the Royal Highland 'holiday home'.

One of the most interesting residues of this era at Ederline is a novel called *The Lady's Walk*, written by 'Mrs Oliphant' (Margaret O. Wilson Oliphant) about Ederline and published in 1897.[26] It is a rather gauzy romance about 'Ellermore' and the kindly ghost who looks after the Campbell family who reside there when they can get away from 'the works' back home. The family is saved from a business collapse and is thus spared the necessity of selling 'Ellermore' by the hero-narrator, inspired by the spirit-lady of the estate. The novel pretends to be nothing other than what it is: light reading for the summer days of the eighteen-nineties. For those who could not even afford a weekend, or were not fortunate enough to be invited to spend the summer with 'the Campbells of Ellermore' or the Bruces of Ederline, they could learn what they were missing by lingering over the pages of *The Lady's Walk*.

There is one passage worth sharing because of the prophetic truth contained in it—truth or irony, or perhaps they are the same—about the temporal quality of possessions:

> . . . nature was as indifferent to the passing away of the human inhabitants, whose little spell of a few hundred years was as nothing in her long history, as she would have been to the falling of a rock on the hillside, or the wrenching up of a tree in the woods. For that matter, of so small account are men, the rock and the tree would both have been older dwellers than the Campbells, and why for that should the sun moderate his shining, or the clear skies veil themselves?[27]

We cannot know whether Mrs Oliphant was referring to the real Campbells who preceded the Bruces, or to the Bruce family, or to neither, but it applied to both, and certainly to the Bruces, whose 'little spell' was considerably less than a few hundred years. In about thirty years (1899) the Bruce family sold the estate to the Warde-Aldams, the grandparents of the present owner, Major William Warde-Aldam of Yorkshire, England. The Bruces would be remembered by several things left by them: the mansion house, begun by the Campbells but finished by the Bruces in 1871, the ruins of which can still be seen; the stained glass windows in Ford Church placed there in memory of members of the family; and the large Celtic cross erected over their graves on the tiny burial island in Loch Ederline which is also the site of the remains of Alexander Duncan Campbell (d. 1841) and William Campbell (d. 1899).

The Warde-Aldams improved the property further, following the example set by the Bruces, and maintained it as a sporting estate. Perhaps because they found it difficult to justify maintaining the estate economically, the Warde-Aldams decided to sell the entire property in 1911, and a beautiful brochure was prepared by agents in advance of the intended sale. (In actual fact, the estate was not sold, but was taken on by the sons [one of whom was the present owner's father] and maintained as a sporting estate for forty years more.)

The prospectus, complete with full-page photographs, gives a detailed picture of what the estate entailed in the early twentieth century.[28] The agricultural lands included not only the grazings and cropland of the 'home farm', but 'Finiecharn' (Finchairn) Farm and Carron and Corrivallich as well, although the total farm acreage is but a fraction of the 13,000 acres belonging to the estate. The buildings include 'a Noble and Spacious Mansion House' of three storeys with twelve bedrooms and dressing rooms, all but one with fireplaces—not counting the three servants' bedrooms—and the inevitable tower. The estate had a nine-hole golf course, its own boat pier on Loch Awe, stables, a sawmill, kennels, several cottages, a boat house, and eight boats on various lochs. The fishing was said to be excellent, and the estate records are said to report 1,112 trout caught in 1903 alone. The shooting was not un-respectable, with 2,370 rabbits killed in 1903, and 727 grouse, and

291 pheasants shot in that same year. The brochure apologizes for the low number of kills between 1907 and 1910, when the game book shows that in this period only 6,673 rabbits, 744 grouse, 108 pheasants, and 11 roe deer were shot.

Like Poltalloch Estate, Ederline employed a large number of farmers, gamekeepers, ghillies (the fishing counterparts of game-keepers), woodcutters, joiners, house servants, and all that were required to keep such a place going. The farms had no crofters on them, but they were tenanted. There were 247 sheep reported on the Home Farm (in contrast with 1,800 today), and 1,400 on the others. Recreation and not agriculture was the major function of the estate from the late nineteenth to the mid-twentieth century, and the employment impact on the Ford area would have reflected this emphasis.

The era of the loch steamers came and went, and so did the time when an estate such as Ederline could be retained for sporting purposes only, or even mainly. Thus, when the estate was turned over to Major Warde-Aldam in the early nineteen-fifties, and particularly when he married in 1960, he says he faced a crucial decision: sell it, or try to keep it up as a sporting estate, or attempt to make a working farm out of it. He chose the last course, not wishing to see the place deteriorate or be acquired by the Forestry Commission and covered with trees. For the past twenty years, the Major has 'rationalized' the estate in order to increase its pro-ductivity and minimize its costs, so that it would come closer to breaking even. The 1871 mansion house is gone, demolished some years back when it was discovered that dry rot had eaten its vitals away, and the Major and his family, who live here about half the year and in Doncaster the rest of it, live in a new, comfortable but unostentatious home overlooking Loch Ederline, built in 1964. (The original estate house, in existence before the mansion was built in 1871, is occupied by the present gamekeeper, Eddie McLean, and his wife.) The Major still enjoys six or eight weekend shoots in the late fall each year, but his main occupation is overseeing the farming and forestry that takes place at Ederline, and on his dairy farm in Doncaster, the profits from which he says make the farm in Argyll possible. He employs five men full-time to help with the operation—the rest is done by casual labour or contractors (as in the case of the timber arrangement), just as in the case of Poltalloch. Major Warde-Aldam thinks the estate may have broken even over the past twenty years, but only because of government policies which provide subsidies for hill farms. (Farming in this area is not really economically feasible, he says, but because it is socially desirable from the point of view of employment, the government encourages agriculture through its programme of subsidies.)

Ederline has thus remained more or less intact, although its uses have changed from post-feudal farming to sporting, and then, since 1960, to 'rationalized' agriculture. It is part of Ford and Ford is part of the estate. The changes which Ederline has undergone have been mirrored in village life, and whatever happens to Ederline in the future will affect the future of the village as well.

Auchinellan

Auchinellan is the smallest of the three estates still extant in Ford, comprising about 730 acres. Like Ederline, it was once in the hands of a branch of the Campbell clan, although a different branch. Unlike both Ederline and Poltalloch, it is not now owner-occupied. It is held in trust in accordance with the will of the last owner, the late James M.B. Wright, until the young heiress to whom he left the estate reaches her majority in about 1991.

An early reference to Campbell ownership appears in the 'Argyll Sasines' thus:

> 3 December 1617: Sasine of the 6 merk lands of Auchinellan and 1 merk land of Corriecraig, in Kilmartin Parish, by Mr. Niall Campbell, rector of Kilmartin, to his lawful son, Mr. Donald Campbell.[29]

Another legal document dated 20 December 1632 seems to confirm ownership by Donald Campbell, who is referred to as the 'minister of Kilmartin', by means of a charter by Lord Lorne.[30] A later document from 1664 seems to suggest that family debts required at least temporary relinquishment of Auchinellan to outsiders:

> 10 May 1664: Sasine of the lands of Auchinellan in Kilmartin Parish, given personally by John Campbell of Auchinellan . . . to John Thomson, merchant burgess of Glasgow, in implement of an obligation . . .[31]

The Campbell connection goes back to the fifteenth century, according to research carried out by the late Mr Wright and recorded in notations in books found in his private library. In fact, 'Dugall, Dean of Argyll', the son of a Sir Colin Campbell, Knight of Lochow who died between 1412 and 1414, is 'the ancestor of Kilmartin and Auchinellan', according to Mr Wright's notes.)[32]

Auchinellan did not remain outside the possession of the Campbells for very long, apparently. In fact, it stayed in the hands of the Donald Campbells for a very long period indeed. In the very first Valuation Rolls for Argyll, in 1855-56, the Proprietor for Auchinellan Estate appears as 'the Heirs of the Revd Donald Campbell of Auchinellan'.[33] (The tenant at this time was one Alexander Jackson.)

The ownership of Auchinellan had changed by 1860-61, however, when the Valuation Rolls show James Reid as Proprietor (with Alexander Jackson remaining as tenant).[34] In 1865-66, James Reid appears as both proprietor and occupier.[35] The same source in 1872-73 indicates that the property is owned by the heirs of James Reid and occupied by an Alexander S. Stevenson.[36]

In 1892-93, the proprietor is listed as 'T.B. Stewart of Pennyland for Auchinellan, for J. and A. Hastie, S.S.C., 5 York Place, Edinburgh'.[37] According to a local history of Ford, the estate was bought in 1922 by the Warde-Aldams of Ederline (the Major's father and his brother) but was immediately sold to a Miss Reid, a descendant of the earlier Campbells of Auchinellan (which may have been the same Reids who earlier had owned it, perhaps having inherited it from the Campbells).[38]

In 1934, Miss Reid's heirs then sold the estate to Mr James M.B. Wright, who through his mother was also distantly related to the Campbells. Mr Wright was also a descendant of the Clark family of Coats and Clark of Paisley, the thread manufacturing firm. He had earlier lived in Inverary, present seat of the Duke of Argyll. Mr Wright, described by his former employees and neighbours as kind, generous, scholarly, and reclusive, was a bachelor. When he died in 1973, the estate was left to the three-year-old grand-daughter of his cousin, who resides in Perthshire. His reasoning can only be guessed at, but Mr Wright appears to have been a deliberate and careful man, especially where things for which he had an affection were concerned, and Auchinellan was something beloved by him. His chief aim was to see that Auchinellan remained in the family for as long as he could make it possible. He may have feared that had he left the property to an older member of the family, none of them having shown any special affection for the place, that they might liquidate it rather promptly, possibly by selling it to the Forestry Commission. Like Major Warde-Aldam and others in the area, Mr Wright probably did not want to see any more of the remaining local land go under trees—Loch Awe had had enough of a good thing long ago. By leaving the estate to his youthful, if distant, relative, Mr Wright could at least protect the property and keep it within the family for another eighteen years beyond his death.

During his lifetime, Mr Wright saw that Auchinellan was used as a productive farm, although he did not oversee it as closely as, say, Major Warde-Aldam. Instead, he left it to his resident farmer/shepherd, Mr Kerr, to see that the place was run properly. He had sufficient wealth that he did not need to be concerned about its profitability, but he did wish to see it productive; his interest was not in sport.

Hamish McNeill came to Auchinellan in 1961 as chauffeur and personal servant to Mr Wright, replacing the recently retired Neil Rowan, who remained in residence on the estate with his wife. At the time he came to work there, the estate employed a chauffeur/valet, a gardener, a daily maid, a housekeeper, a farm manager, and a farmhand (five full-time and one part-time). Now there is only Hamish McNeill, employed on a part-time basis as the resident caretaker.

The estate is not deserted or unused, however. Mr Wright generously made provision in his will for the people who had worked for him at Auchinellan. The McNeills, who live with their two teenaged children in the bungalow built for them by Mr Wright, have a life interest in that property and continue to live on the estate. The late Mrs Rowan, widow of the retired chauffeur, was provided her cottage on the estate for her lifetime, as is Mrs Kerr, widow of the farm manager. Thus a total of five people live in a cluster of three homes up the hill from the big house at Auchinellan. In addition, the farmland is leased to Nigel Boase, Lunga, who has for the past two years hired Geordie McKenzie from the island of

Mull as shepherd over both Auchinellan and Creaganterve lands. There are presently 300 sheep and 24 cows on the land, not including the 12 sheep kept by Hamish McNeill with the help of the late Mr Kerr's collie, Rona.

No one associated with it today really wants to guess what the future of Auchinellan will be. In the distant past its owners provided important leadership in the parish, and in the recent past and in the present the people who live there have been very important participants in the life of the village of Ford, and the land has been and is still in productive use. The question no one can answer, including and perhaps especially the young beneficiary herself, is what will become of the old estate when the late Mr Wright's beneficiary enjoys her twenty-first birthday in a few more years. (Her visits to the estate with her family are said to be infrequent, not only because of the inconvenience of a drive from Perth to the West Highlands, but because she suffers from carsickness and simply cannot enjoy the trip. One hopes this malady will not influence her affection for the place. On such unexpected, chance trivia the fates of principalities turn. Even the ancient Sir Colin Campbell, let alone James M.B. Wright, could not prepare for every small eventuality.)

The Village of Ford

The very earliest history of the village of Ford is by now difficult to recover. Most of what is known has been included in an excellent local history called *Ford and District*, a 51-page book prepared by the Scottish Women's Rural Institute in Ford in about 1966.[39]

No doubt the village grew in part because it was located at the conjunction of the three estates of Ederline, Auchinellan, and Poltalloch, and it provided a place of residence for a number of families who provided labour and services for one or another (or all three) of these estates.

But, as mentioned earlier, the best clue to the origin of Ford is probably in the name itself, which derives from the fact that it is located precisely at the sites of the two fords (neither of which exist presently) across the tiny river which empties into Loch Awe at its southernmost point. The ford was important as a major crossing point for carriages and for livestock, located as it was on a drove-road and carriageway which took traffic from the Western Isles and Oban past the southern end of Loch Awe and thence past Finchairn Farm and the old Kilineuair Church over the mountains to Loch Fyne. It is no doubt this road, and its importance in the seventeenth, eighteenth and nineteenth centuries, which accounts for the presence of a village at this shallow place in the river.

The road, still called locally 'the drove road', appears on a map published in 1845 as the main route from Oban to both Kilmartin and to a place on Loch Fyne near Inverary, at the farm called Auchendrain—the road directly from Kilmartin to Oban apparently had not yet been built.[40]

Haldane's books on the early roads in Scotland leave little doubt about the importance of the tracks which went through Ford and near it. He says

> ... perhaps the most important (road) started from where the little ruined chapel of Kilineuair still stands two miles east of Ford leading south-east across the hills through the stretch of country known at one time as the Leckan Muir to Auchendrain three miles north of Furnace on Loch Fyne.[41]

Not only were drovers seen frequently on this road bringing cattle from Mull and Lorn to the lowland trysts, or markets at Falkirk and Stirling, but 'because the woods around Loch Awe and Loch Etive supplied the fuel and the charcoal for the local smelting industry' it was not unusual from the mid-eighteenth century and well into the nineteenth century to see 'strings of ponies loaded with charcoal ... crossing the hills to the south of Loch Awe'.[42]

At one time in the nineteenth century, according to Haldane,

> Ambitious plans were ... put forward for roads crossing the high ground both north and south of Loch Awe, including the improvement of "that much frequented path" by which the people of North Lorn and certain of the Islands had long been accustomed to take their cattle across the Leckan Muir from Ford on Loch Awe to Inverary on their way to the markets of the Lowlands.[43]

But even further back in history, says Haldane, these tracks are thought to have been used 'from the early days of Scotland's history by kings and nobles, monks and pilgrims in days when Iona was still the spiritual centre of Scotland and the burial-place of her kings'.[44]

(This claim is not as far-fetched as it might sound, considering that Kilineuair Church, now a ruin, was once a mission outpost from Iona and is believed to have been begun by St Columba himself. The church was still active in the Middle Ages—three Vatican documents are known which make reference to it in 1422 and 1423.[45] Sometime in the late Middle Ages the centre of religious activities was shifted to Kilmartin. Kilineuair ceased to be used for worship in the late 1500s, but the burial ground was used as late as the 1950s.)[46]

Travel by notables through the area on these roads did not cease in ancient times, incidentally. Keats came through Ford on a walking tour with a friend in 1818 and is said to have spent the night at the Change-house, and the Wordsworths and Coleridge came up the old road from Inverary to the north end of Loch Awe in 1803.

Although the name 'Ford' is English (spelled 'Foord' in some documents from the late seventeenth and eighteenth centuries), suggesting a rather late date for the settling of the village, the original name for the place is the Gaelic *Ath nan Cnoc*, or 'the ford of the hazels', indicating that the place-name became anglicized long after it had been established as a recognized site during more 'Gaelic' times.

A legal transaction recorded in 1694 shows, for example, that 'the Ford of Anagra' (an English attempt to write *Ath nan Cnoc*) was well known in at least the seventeenth century:

> 30th April 1694: Acknowledgement by David McCallum brother german to Poltalloch that he has received from Donal McCallum bailie of Glasrie his uncle 900 merks for which he is to give cows and stots conform to their bargain and to deliver them at the Ford of Anagra before 20th May 1694.[47]

Fifty years later the minutes of the Commissioners of Supply for Argyll make mention of 'Dougald Campbell change-keeper at Anacra, at the Ford', who was appointed to oversee the roadwork required by inhabitants of Salachry and Kintraw. In the 1745 minutes, mention is made of 'the Ford of Anacraw'.[48]

From these records we can establish not only that Ford was a recognized place over three hundred years ago, but that at least by the middle of the eighteenth century there was commercial activity there: the change-house referred to was a stable and an inn which provided a fresh change of horses and overnight accommodation for the drover and carriage traffic of those years. A smithy has existed at Ford probably for as many years as change-houses, and a cattle-stance was located across from the present Ford Hotel for overnight grazing of cattle being driven to market. The minutes from 1745 also make an important reference to 'the Schooll at the Foord, where one had been kept a long time', a school which was said to be equal in size to that of Kilmartin. Where there was a school we can be certain there was a community of some kind, with families and children in sufficient number to justify the appointment of a master or dominie (no doubt by the church).

The *Statistical Account of Scotland* provides some interesting glimpses of life in Kilmartin Parish in the late eighteenth century.[49] The population of the parish, said to be 1,150 in 1755, has grown to 1,537 by 1794, mostly cotters and tenants, with a few crofters (24 families) remaining. There are 1,800 black cattle and 6,000 sheep. One hundred thousand trees have been planted on one property in the past 25 years, perhaps presaging the massive forestry plantings of the twentieth century. The fishing in Loch Awe 'has not hitherto been so very productive, as to make it an object worthy of much public notice', a situation which will change in a few decades. Smallpox has almost been eliminated by inoculation, but 'hooping cough' is said to be exceedingly severe. Kilmartin is the only village mentioned (perhaps the minister writing the account felt it was the only settlement worthy of the name). It held three markets a year, one for cattle and two for horses. Peat was the main fuel used, but it was hoped that the proposed Crinan Canal would make coals (and salt) available to the parish,[50] and it was further hoped that an additional canal would be built to Loch Awe.

The writer laments that proprietors of arable farms do not make more improvements upon them, and observes that the short leases (seven to nine years) provide no incentives for tenants to make such improvements. About the people he writes that they are 'of a middling size, squat, and pretty strong made, though not very remarkable for extraordinary strength'. He finds that the few gentry 'live genteelly, without being extravagant', and the other class 'are economists from necessity; their only luxury being a little whisky occasionally, which excites some mirth and glee.'

Interestingly, every inhabitant of the parish but for two shepherds is said to be native to Kilmartin and neighbouring parishes, a situation which changed drastically in the twentieth century. Only three families had emigrated to America in thirty years, and a few young men had gone to the lowlands for work, although they generally returned soon. This kind of stability, too, will change. 'The language commonly spoken, is the Gaelic, . . . though the English is generally a little understood even by the common people, and spoken by many'. The economy is not a commercial one, and 'money is slow in its circulation'.

Eleven 'Taylors' and 16 weavers were counted among the population, along with 4 smiths, 4 carpenters, 6 shoemakers, 22 men servants, 29 servants, 4 millers, and one wheelwright, cart maker, ferryman, and salmon fisher. About twenty young men went north for the fishing every year—there was no herring fishing in the parish itself. No mention is made of the land clearances as such, but pasturage was said to have been increased, causing the dispossession of around forty families of tenants in the 1770s, and this can only mean that people were removed to make room for either sheep or cattle or both. Most of the 'former possessors', however, were kept on as cotters so that they could be returned to tillage if needed in the future, and thus 'the loss which population would otherwise sustain, is, in a considerable degree, made up'.

There must have been little relief from privation, hard work, and disease in these times. A letter from John Campbell of Echlie, a croft at the Ford, to his uncle Archibald in 1825 tells of the death of his father, who died seven weeks after he was 'struck by a pain in his back taking a creel of peats to the kiln for the purpose of drying corn. Dr. (John) McKellar thought it to be a fever which has been very prevalent in the Highlands this year'.[51] Echlie is nothing today but the barest remains—a few stones mark the site of the croft and the kiln at the foot of Dun Dubh. No doctor lives in Ford today, and indeed, the village was unusual in its good fortune in having a doctor in residence 160 years ago. Although the purpose of John Campbell's letter is to tell of his father's going 'to the bosom of Abraham', space was given at the end for a report on the sheep and the rent.

Sheep, black cattle, and horses seem to have been the main

portion of the estate of Neil Campbell of Dunchragaig—these are the most prominent items listed by him in his handwritten will sent to his son Donald in 1825.[52] Donald, born in 1873, married the year after this will was made, and soon thereafter moved with his wife to Ford, where the family operated a farm and a change-house from 1836 to 1849. A few pages of the change-house account book survived the Campbells' emigration to America in 1853.[53] The entries from this book suggest that many a sorrow was drowned at the change-house with a mutchkin of ale or a gill or two of whisky. (In actuality, more good times were celebrated than sad times drowned, as in the case of Archibald McIntyre, gamekeeper, who was charged 2 shillings for two half mutchkins (half pints) when his child was baptised in July, 1843.) Curiously but prophetically, the last words entered on the last page of the account book in 1849 are 'Come to this happy land Come Come Away', a tune which was to become very popular in the Sacred Harp shape-note tradition in America.

While Donald Campbell was operating the farm and the change-house at Ford, his nephew, Donald Jackson (the minister who later helped organize the church at Ford), seems to have taken an interest in him and the rest of the family there. He wrote to his brother Archibald Campbell in 1840:

> How does Donald get on at Ford? Barbara is active enough but I fear Donald is a bad waiter. He must not sit and drink with the people. It would only be to acquire a bad habit. He was not by nature intended for an inn keeper so he should leave the management of the house to his wife and look well after the business of the farm.[54]

He is full of questions about the markets held earlier that year, about the possibility of expanding the farmland worked by Archibald, about his new house, and about how handily his pony takes him from house to house throughout the parish so that he can hold services up and down the 25 miles of it. He also takes this opportunity to encourage Archibald to improve his mind, asking 'How do you mean to spend the long winter nights?' and then suggesting that he take up the reading of history and subscribe to a weekly newspaper 'that you may know the state of the world.' If a pound is too much to pay for a year's papers, then the reverend suggests Archibald can get a 'second reading' of it for half price.

The concerns of people in the area are much the same 14 years later when George Campbell writes from Ardefuir to his brother Donald in America, having just learned that Donald reached his destination safely the year before.[55] The letter is filled with news of the markets and of cattle and sheep prices, of the wet weather which almost ruined the entire harvest of hay, of the most recent shearing, of all the local deaths from cholera, of the loss of 420 lives when a shipload of emigrees bound for Australia went down in Dublin Bay, and of the local stabbings and assorted mayhem. Almost breathlessly, George writes of all the births and deaths at Salachry, Ederline, Inverliever, and a dozen other farms and estates, and even tells the gossip about Alina at Kintraw who plans to marry a widower from Glasgow 'but the whole of her friends is against her she left Kintraw she staying with her Uncle I do not mind of more news just now but you will get the whole in my next . . .'

The *New Statistical Account* published in 1845 makes specific mention of Ford in the section on Kilmartin Parish.[56] Four markets are held yearly in the parish, the minister reports, two of them at 'the Ford'. He records that there are two change-houses in the parish, 'the two public houses at the Ford, which are more orderly and better provided than formerly'. About the people of the parish generally, the minister says 'There are no insane, fatuous, deaf, or dumb persons in the parish, or belonging to it.' He also observes that Gaelic 'is preferred by all the natives', but 'it is fast losing ground, particularly among the young people', a statement which contrasts somewhat with the account fifty years earlier.

Of the ten 'old proprietors' said to be important to the history of the parish, only three are still in possession of their lands in 1845: Malcolm of Poltalloch, MacLachlan of Creaganterve, and Campbell of Auchinellan. (The Campbells of Ederline were still there, but in the neighbouring parish of Glassary.) We do not know precisely what the housing was like in Ford, but there is a clue in this description of nearby Kilmartin:

> The village of Kilmartin has been entirely rebuilt and remodelled within the last few years. Instead of the rude and ill-assorted thatched cottages, all of which are now removed, the proprietor has put down substantial slated cottages, having garden and shrubbery ground enclosed and railed in for each, the whole having an air of neatness and comfort formerly unknown in this part of the country.

These improvements were probably not enjoyed by Ford for many years, judging from pictures of the Ford Post Office at the turn of the century, which show it with the traditional thatched roof.

The 1845 *Statistical Account* gives the population of the parish as 1,213 for the year 1841.[57] In 1843 there were 25 new births and 8 marriages. The decrease in population was attributed to emigration to America and to the enlargement and improvement of farms.[58] The minister observed that drunkenness, quarrelling, poaching, and smuggling were comparatively rare now.

Several new breeds of cattle and sheep had been introduced, and drainage of bogs and other agricultural improvements were taking place. The growing of turnips and potatoes was said to be extensive. Eighty-six hundred sheep and 1,976 cattle grazed the land.

Fifty-two men were employed in farming this year, and another 117 as farm servants, labourers, and shepherds. There were 40 cotters and only 9 crofters left in the parish by this time. Fifty-three tradesmen and apprentices were in the parish, 23 'boys employed in herding', and 39 female servants. The number of poor receiving parochial aid was said to be 26.

The minister lamented the absence of 'middlemen or gentlemen farmers' in the parish, believing that the resulting gap between the landlord and the people resulted in 'jealousy, distrust, and discontent', but he seemed generally pleased with the improvements made in agriculture and living standards.

The last third of the nineteenth century saw the development of sporting activities around Loch Awe. Ederline Estate (and to a lesser extent Poltalloch's Inverliever) was converted into a sporting estate, and steamers began to ply the Loch bringing passengers to Ford for the enjoyment of fishing, shooting and the scenery.[59] The Auchinellan Inn was built in 1864, possibly on the site of one of the earlier change-houses. This building was eventually improved and expanded into the present Ford Hotel. The Ford Gun Club was active in 1880, and a photograph from that year still hangs in the Ford Hotel, revealing the proud hirsute visages of 64 men with their guns and their Victorian-era shooting togs.

In addition to the shepherds and farmers, the smith, the change-house keepers, servants, weavers, and others who for generations had made a living in and around Ford, gamekeepers and ghillies found employment there in swelling numbers toward the end of the century.

According to the *Ford and District* history, residents of Ford around the turn of the century found much to enjoy there. School children enjoyed Saturdays when they could walk to the pierhead and watch the S.S. *Loch Awe* sail in to discharge its passengers into the waiting horse-drawn coach. The school drew children from all ages from a wide area, some walking the old drove road from Salachry. A Gaelic choir competed in the Mod in Lochgilphead. The Ford Fair was 'held on the ground beside the river when farmers paraded their well groomed horses around the village and business deals were transacted—the Hotel being their focal point.'[60] Hogmanay (the festival of New Year) was a special time for visiting, for enjoying food and drink and friendship.

Pheasants multiplied on the hills where they could find cover, having been introduced into the Highlands in the mid-nineteenth century and nurtured by gamekeepers hired for that purpose. The fish in Loch Awe began to attract attention for their size and number, some of them having also been introduced from stocking ponds at Ederline. Game books and fishing logs registered the incredible number of kills enjoyed by sportsmen who either came to Ford as guests of estates or stayed at the Hotel and leased the shooting and fishing by the day or week.

Despite this shift to sport, however, the hills were more thickly populated by sheep (and some cattle) than by pheasants, grouse, deer, and sportsmen. Sport and recreation made an important adjunctive enterprise to the predominant economic base of Ford, which continued to be agriculture.

While sport continued to boom, and to put Ford on the map in a way it had never enjoyed before (at least, perhaps, since the days of Kilineuair), the new century brought with it changes which would gradually reduce the importance of agriculture. The most important new element was forestry.

The Office of Woods began planting on the mixed hill grazing and sporting estate of Inverliever, which it had bought from Poltalloch, within two years of the purchase in 1907. This was the first major planting by the government anywhere in Scotland, which is one of the reasons Argyll has one of the oldest developed forestry plantations in the United Kingdom. After World War One, when the government recognized wood as a strategic war material, it created the Forestry Commission in 1919 with the express charge of rapid and extensive afforestation. A review of the early experience of this forest carried out at Inverliever resulted in recommendations which served as a blueprint for forestry policy and practice in the area for many years.[61] The new Forestry Commission bought up additional lands around Loch Awe as well as elsewhere throughout the United Kingdom, and it took over Inverliever from its predecessor agency in 1924. The sheep around Loch Awe began to decline in number as the tree plantations expanded. The change was noticeable to those who returned for visits. Said one:

> Ford's physical features have not changed much over the years with the exception of wooded slopes where once only sheep and cattle grazed.[62]

The change was not so sudden or drastic as it might appear in retrospect, although its significance can hardly be underestimated. The old Office of Woods was charged with finding a better use for hill land than the sheep and cattle grazing which had been tried for 200 years with marginal results. It was thought that the new forests would make productive use of the land and provide employment, thus stabilizing the population on the land. Planting was not entirely new to the area—as already noted, afforestation was being carried out elsewhere in the parish before 1845, possibly with the same purposes in mind as the Office of Woods espoused, but more likely for profit. The mission of the new Forestry Commission was somewhat different from that of the Office of Woods, but, at least in principle, neither of them consciously set out to remove farmers or sheep from the land. In reviewing the history of Inverliever Forest in 1953, the Commission stated that

> the Estate was given over almost entirely to sheep and cattle grazing and it was essential in order to keep these farms going as economic units to allocate to them a certain amount of plantable land. Further areas of good land were also allocated towards the formation of small holdings.[63]

Out of the 12,600 acres contained on the estate, 5,200 acres were declared suitable for further forestry plantation, and of this number, 2,000 acres were set aside for the continuation of farming. Some of this acreage is still farmed today. The Commission reckoned that compared to the stock held in 1907, the numbers in 1953 had fallen, but not drastically, and the number of cattle had even increased.[64] The current stock population in this area is around 1,800 sheep and 140 cows.

While the stated and conscious intention of the Forestry Commission was not to supplant hill farming where it could be productive, it may have had this long-term effect in the vicinity of Loch Awe; although for Argyll as a whole and for the Southwest Conservancy there is no inverse relationship between acreage under plantation and the numbers of sheep and cattle produced between 1920 and the mid-1970s.[65] (That is, for the larger area around Loch Awe, the increase in Forestry Commission planting does not seem to have brought about a decrease in the number of sheep and cattle—both were on the increase through the mid-1970s.) But on Loch Awe itself, while there are no firm figures readily available, sheep production does appear to have gone down while the acreage under trees has grown dramatically. In 1925, only 75 acres had been planted in Inverliever Forest, while in 1980 the number was over 21,000 acres. When the acreage for the three forests of Inverliever, Inverinan, and Eredine are combined, the total for the lochside is almost 33,000. The forest has expanded to about 50 square miles on the northwestern shore alone.[66] It is almost inevitable, given the amount of land devoted to afforestation, that livestock, (mainly sheep) would be displaced.

The consequences for the structure of employment in the area of Ford in this century are obvious. Opportunities for forestry planting jobs increased here, paralleling the rapid growth of forestry jobs throughout the United Kingdom. In 1920 there were 935 forest workers in the U.K.; by 1949 the number had grown to over 12,000.[67] Simultaneously, the number of agricultural workers decreased, a nearly-universal trend operating quite independently of developments in forestry, and more closely associated with the general depopulation of rural areas. In Argyll, in 1937, there were 3,470 persons employed on agricultural holdings; their number steadily dwindled to 1,262 in 1978.[68] (The number of agricultural holdings in Argyll also decreased—from around 3,000 in 1938 to just over 1,300 in 1975—suggesting again that agricultural employment was lost as land use was transferred from farming to other purposes, including forestry.)[69]

The Forestry Commission's 1953 history of the Inverliever Forest complains that until the preceding year forestry labour was in very short supply. Three-fifths of the area had reached thinning stage; thinning and essential maintenance work were both being delayed for lack of manpower. Then in 1952 the Commission opened new housing in its 'created' village at Dalavich. Thirty-seven new houses were built here, and more housing was subsequently built at Ford (four Forestry houses had been placed here between the wars and six more were built in Ford after World War Two) and in the new village of Eredine on the opposite lochside. (The Forestry villages and new housing at Ford were constructed in response to a postwar explosion in forestry employment, which practically doubled in the U.K. between 1945 and 1949. But the new housing was accomplished just in time for a sharp and steady decline in forestry work in Scotland, which fell from 4,738 in 1955 to 4,105 in 1960 and 2,965 in 1970.[70]

The commission provides interesting data on population changes at Inverliever between 1908 and 1952.[71] In 1908, according to Forestry Commission figures, there were 55 persons residing on the estate, 43 of whom were associated with farming in one way or another—22 were males, 11 were children. In 1912, eighty-seven people lived on the former estate, 38 of whom were associated with forestry. There were 35 males and 27 children. Most of the early labour force recruitment was done locally, according to the report, but workers were brought in from outside as the volume of work increased. (The report also describes the employment of females and conscientious objectors during World War One when forestry lost men to the armed services.)

In 1952, forty years after the last figures were assembled, 285 people were residing at Inverliever Forest (an additional 9 were employed there but residing elsewhere). Of these 285 people, only 27 were in farming families, while 232 were employed in afforestation. Eighty-nine were males, and there were 111 children. As already suggested, the early 1950s seem to have been the peak employment period for the Forestry Commission. The introduction of the power saw, the replacement of horses with tractors, and the improvement of winching technology meant that more work could be accomplished with fewer human hands. Consequently, the labour force at Inverliever in the late 1950s was only 101,[72] and in 1981 stood at only 30, but these 30 employees were said to be sufficient to carry out all the planting, all the restocking, and the production needed to supply 15,000 tons of timber yearly to (mainly foreign) timber and pulpwood yards.[73] The extent of forestry, timbering and timber-related employment in the area of Argyll was and is, of course, much larger than that included in the Forestry Commission's domain. It is generally agreed that privately-owned forest land and the labour and produce associated with it would be about equal to those connected with the Commission.

The decline in forestry employment was happily timed with an increase in motoring holiday-makers, brought onto the lochside by improved roads. Tourism increased as forestry employment fell, and the Commission eventually moved into the recreation business by renting foresters' vacant houses to holiday-makers. The excess housing, including that in Ford, was also rented to any suitable permanent resident, so that the Forestry Commission was, and is, also in the local housing business as well as in tourism. (The increased interest in tourism was attributed by local people to interest in scenery. Fishing no longer attracted visitors to Loch Awe because it had been overfished.[74] According to another popular theory, the salmon had declined since the Ben Cruachan Power Station was built, placing impediments in the way of spawning salmon.)

In preparation for Fraser Darling's milestone work, *The West Highland Survey*, Field Survey Officer Colin P. MacDonald visited Ford on 8 August 1948. Copies of his original field notes are still available in the Scottish Records Office and in the library of the Highlands and Islands Development Board. The notes from Ford provide us with an abbreviated picture of the village as it was seen by this visiting social observer. The laird was given by Mr MacDonald as 'Foresty Commission'. The school contained 17 children; there were no other social organizations listed besides the church. Part-time work was available in forestry and 'ghillieing'. Communications included twice weekly bus service to Ardrishaig, a post office, and a telephone kiosk. Coal and wood were used for fuel. The farming was classified as non-crofting. On the back of the note card, Mr MacDonald wrote:

> Ford is a tiny, rather isolated hamlet at the head of Loch Awe (one of the few free-angling lochs in the Highlands) and consists of an hotel, school, post office, church (C of S) and 4 or 5 other cottages. It is non-crofting but the residents are mostly forestry workers and some find employment as ghillies during the season. The surrounding country is uneven but green and fertile and the Forestry Commission now own much of it. Quite a lot has been planted with the usual conifers and there is even a forestry nursery taking advantage of the rich red loam near the hamlet.

The Kilmartin Parish section of the *Third Statistical Account of Scotland* was prepared in its final version in 1955.[75] The writer, Revd Angus MacLeod, reviews the changes in population which transpired from 1801 to 1951, and concludes that the continued decline was caused by 'an obsolescent economy' and the too-drastic reduction in the number of small farm holdings. He comments on the recent building of more housing in the future.

The church in Ford is also mentioned, but most attention is given to the Kilmartin church, where Gaelic services are held once a month for about fifteen parishioners. 'Gaelic is falling out of use not only for worship', says the Revd MacLeod, 'but also for colloquial purposes: very few parishioners speak it correctly or fluently, much less read and write it.'

His description of education in the parish includes reference to the one-teacher school at Ford. Agriculture is said to remain the major industry in the parish, but the Inverliever plantings by the Forestry Commission are said to offer good employment for the young men of the parish, 'and consequently there is no unemployment, though some of them naturally have other ambitions and prefer to go to the big cities to seek their fortune.' Many services are now procured from towns such as Lochgilphead, and the only tradesmen in the parish in 1955 are a plumber, a joiner, and a tailor. Most wants are supplied by mobile vans or by driving to the towns.

There is said to be no crime and no juvenile delinquency, and there are no 'real poor' among the parishioners. The minister concludes that '. . . the means towards the enjoyment of a happy social life [are] quite unstinted. No age is neglected, and the whole community lives in an atmosphere of contented rural life.'

More recent population figures for the parish indicate, however, that the number of people in the parish did not stabilize as the Revd MacLeod had hoped (see Table 1, Chapter V). Few material fortunes were to be found in the 1950s and 1960s in the Mid-Argyll area, even in forestry, and the flow of native people from the area to the cities of Scotland and England, as well as to other countries, continued. From the peak of 1,537 persons reported in 1794 for Kilmartin parish, the number declined steadily through the nineteenth and twentieth centuries until 1971, when the figure was 327. (The preliminary figure for 1981 provided by the District Council Office indicates, however, that the population has increased in the past ten years.)

Contrary to the picture of 'contented rural life' painted by the minister in 1955, places such as Ford were facing, or were about to face, serious problems of survival. Farming, tourism, and forestry still offered a livelihood for some, but opportunities for making a living seem to have shrunk rather than expanded in the decades following the last *Statistical Account*. To be sure, progress came to Ford in the form of improved transportation and communication. Electricity came to the village in 1963. Piped water became available in 1964. Adequate television reception was made possible in 1977 when a community group erected a workable cable system. A village hall was built in 1968 and a new grocery shop was erected. The old farmhouse at Torran Mor was converted into eight modern council flats. Regarding all these achievements there is obvious and justifiable pride amongst the people of Ford.

But could the fundamental problem of depopulation be solved? Could the community withstand the loss of important institutions such as the school, which closed in the early 1970s, and the reduced importance of the church, whose active membership dwindled to about a dozen? Could it withstand the cultural changes such as the passing of Gaelic speakers (out of a population of 109 reported in 1966, 14 are said to be Gaelic speakers;[76] in 1981 there are 6) and changes in traditional forms of work? Could it in fact withstand its own absorption into the mainstream of Scottish, British, and world life without losing a sense of itself as unique? Will Ford, and places like it in the West Highlands, survive on maps of the future only as memories, or worse, as living corpses? The future of any social creature so complex as a human community is not easily foretold, but at least a response to these intimations of eclipse can be made if we first understand the structures and social life of the village and then assess the recent changes experienced by Ford, examining the reactions of the community to them.

Footnotes

[1]A brief but apparently accurate account of Mid-Argyll's early history and the remains visible today can be found in N.H. Murray's respected *The Companion Guide to the West Highlands of Scotland*, London: Collins, 1977 (7th edition), pp.72-85.

[2]J.R.N. McPhail, ed., *Highland Papers*, Vol.II (Edinburgh: University Press for the Scottish Historical Society, 1916), p. 121n.

[3]*Scotland: Owners of Lands and Heritages, 1872-73 Return* (Edinburgh: Murray and Gibb, 1874), p. 15.

[4]Henry M. Paton (compiler), *The Malcolms of Poltalloch, 1530-1923* (London: Sangorski and Sutcliffe, Binders, 1927).

[5]Valuation Rolls of County of Argyll, 1855-56, 1860-61, 1865-66, 1872-73, 1880-81, 1892-93, Scottish Record Office, Edinburgh.

[6]Kilmartin Parish Kirk Session Minutes, 1694-1895, Scottish Record Office, Edinburgh.

[7]*Statistical Account of Scotland, County of Argyll*, 1794, 'Kilmartin Parish'.

[8]Description of the Loch Aweside Canal, dated 1793, found in the Poltalloch papers in the Argyll and Bute District Council Archives,

Kilmory House, Lochgilphead.

[9]These plans, dated 1864, are found in the Poltalloch papers housed in the Scottish Records Office, Edinburgh.

[10]Excerpt from copy of the original handwritten deed in the possession of Thomas Alston of Ford. Other lands which went to the Office of Woods in this exchange included Dalavich, Arinachtan, Corridowlochan, Cruachan, Arivoldonich, Ardekulkechan, Corribuie, Corrychraig, and Barmaddy. (The language of these Scottish legal documents is irresistibly humorous to those unfamiliar with it. This deed refers at one point to 'houses biggings yards tofts crofts outsetts sheallings grassings mosses muirs meadows woods parts pendicles and pertinents thereof', a phrase which I find as interesting for its metre as for its meaning.

[11]'Prospectus on Poltalloch Property to be Sold at Auction on 9, 10, 11 September, 1954'. Prepared by John D. Wood and Co. (Auctioneers), London.

[12]Hubert Fenwick, *Scotland's Castles* (London: Robert Hale, 1976), p. 178.

[13]The level of bank lending to Scottish farmers has alarmed some observers who find that agricultural borrowing has increased by 260 per cent in the last five years, and that 'farming is being financed from borrowing, not from income', a 'desperate state of affairs'. ['Bank Lendings Continue to Rise', *Scottish Farming Leader* (August 1981), p.19; 'Interest Charges', *Scottish Farming Leader* (February 1981), p. 19.]

[14]Committee of the Royal Scottish Geographical Society, *The Early Maps of Scotland*, 3rd edition (Edinburgh: The Royal Scottish Geographical Society, 1973), pp. 52, 84, 101, and frontispiece-facsimile of Blaeu map in the Scottish Record Office, Edinburgh.

[15]J.R.N. McPhail, ed., *Highland Papers*, Vol. II (Edinburgh: University Press for the Scottish Historical Society, 1916), pp. 136-138.

[16]*Ibid.*, p. 121.

[17]Herbert Campbell, *Abstracts of the Particular Register of Sasines for Argyll, Bute, and Dunbarton Otherwise Known as the Argyll Sasines* (Edinburgh: W. Brown, Ltd., 1933), p. 27.

[18]Thomas Pennant, *A Tour in Scotland, 1772* (London: Benjamin

White, 1790); Michael Brander, *The Making of the Highlands* (London: Constable, 1980); Margaret Olympia Campbell, *A Memorial History of the Simmons and Bolten*, 1882.

[19]Patrick H. Gillies, *Netherlorn, Argyllshire, and Its Neighbourhood* (London: Virtue and Col, 1909).

[20]Herbert Campbell, *op. cit.*, p. 338; Henry M. Paton (compiler) *op. cit.*, p. 130.

[21]G. Harvey Johnston, *The Heraldry of the Campbells*, Vol. I (Edinburgh: W. and A.K. Johnston, Ltd., 1920), p. 73.

[22]*The New Statistical Account of Scotland*, Vol. VII (Renfrew and Argyll), (Edinburgh: William Blackwood and Sons, 1845).

[23]Valuation Rolls, *Argyll*, 1855-56, 1860-61, 1865-66.

[24]*Scotland: Owners of Lands and Heritages*, p. 11.

[25]Philip Gaskell, *Morvern Transformed: A Highland Parish in the Nineteenth Century* (Cambridge: Cambridge University Press, 1980) (2nd ed.).

[26]Mrs Oliphant, *The Lady's Walk* (London: Methuen, 1897).

[27]*Ibid.*, pp. 154-155.

[28]'Particulars of the Estate of Ederline, Argyllshire', printed at the Edinburgh University Press circa 1911, 22 pp., in the possession of Major W. Warde-Aldam.

[29]*Argyll Sasines, op. cit.*, p. 5.

[30]*Ibid.*, p. 141. Donald Campbell is elsewhere said to be the first Presbyterian minister in Kilmartin, but in 1639. See *New Statistical Account of Scotland* Vol. VII, *op. cit.*, p. 565.

[31]*Ibid.*, p. 376.

[32]Notation found on p. 18 of G. Harvey Johnston, *op. cit.* Mr Wright supports his conclusion with a reference to 'Highland Papers', Vol. IV, Scottish History Society, p. 177.

[33]Valuation Rolls, Argyll, 1855-56.

[34]Valuation Rolls, 1860-61.

[35]Valuation Rolls, 1965-66.

[36]Valuation Rolls, 1972-73.

[37]Valuation Rolls, 1892-93.

[38]*Ford and District*, prepared by the Ford S.W.R.I. (Oban: *Oban Times*, n.d., circa 1966), p. 16.

[39]*Ford and District*, prepared by the Ford S.W.R.I. (Oban: *Oban Times,* n.d., circa 1966). This important local history was prepared by fifteen women from Ford with the assistance of accomplished experts on the history of the area, including the late Alasdair Carmichael and Miss Marion Campbell.

[40]*The New Statistical Account of Scotland*, Vol VII (Renfrew and Argyll), (Edinburgh: William Blackwood and Sons, 1845), map facing p. 1. This map shows a crossroads where Ford is located, with one road running from Kilmartin to Taynuilt, and another running from Kintraw and Ashranish to Loch Fyneside. The village of Ford does not appear on this map, but earlier records indicate that it had been there as a recognized place for many decades.

[41]A.R.B. Haldane, *The Drove Roads of Scotland* (London: Thomas Nelson and Sons, 1953), p. 90.

[42]*Ibid.*, p. 91.

[43]A.R.B. Haldane, *New Ways Through the Glens: Highland Road, Bridge, and Canal Makers of the Early Nineteenth Century* (Newton Abbott: David and Charles, 1962), p. 67. This plan was never implemented.

[44]Haldane, *Drove Roads, op. cit.,* p. 89.

[45]J.R.N. McPhail, ed., *Highland Papers,* Vol. IV (Edinburgh: University Press, 1934), pp. 177-8, and *Ford and District, op. cit.,* p. 9.

[46]*Ford and District, op. cit.,* p. 9; correspondence from Mrs Athole Cameron to Sheena Carmichael, n.d.

[47]Abstract from Henry M. Paton (compiler), *The Malcolms of Poltalloch, op. cit.,* pp. 122-123.

[48]Minutes of the Commissioners of Supply for Argyll, 2 June 1744 and 6 June 1745, in the Archives of Argyll and Bute District Council, Kilmory, Lochgilphead.

[49]*Statistical Account of Scotland,* Vol. 13 (1794). The Kilmartin Parish report is written by the Revd Mr Hugh Campbell.

[50]*Ibid.*, p. 94: '. . . if the duty were taken off the (coal) and rock salt allowed to be imported, the people is these countries would be as happy as they are now miserable, and they would be under no temptation of leaving their native soil, to try their fortunes in America.'

[51]Letter obtained from Sheena Carmichael.

[52]Copy of this will in the possession of Sheena Carmichael.

[53]From Sheena Carmichael.

[54]Document in the possession of Sheena Carmichael.

[55]Document in the possession of Sheena Carmichael.

[56]*The New Statistical Account of Scotland*, Vol. VII (Renfrew and Argyll), (Edinburgh: William Blackwood and Sons, 1845). The Revd Donald McCalman prepared the Kilmartin Parish report.

[57]*The New Statistical Account of Scotland, op. cit.,* p. 561.

[58]Scholars such as Eric Cregeen and James Hunter agree that such emigration was not caused by wholesale evictions, or 'clearances' for which other areas of the Highlands became famous. (From conversations with Cregeen and Hunter, Autumn, 1981.)

[59]*Ford and District,* p. 27.

[60]There were nineteen steamers on Loch Awe between the years 1861 and 1952, many of which were operated by David MacBrayne and his predecessor. The first steamer was the *Eva* (1861-62), the second was the *Queen of the Lake* (1863-73). One of the last was the *Countess (of Breadalbane) II* (1936-51). For a complete account, see C.L.D. Duckworth and G.E. Langmuir, *Clyde River and Other Steamers,* 3rd ed. (Glasgow: Brown, Son, and Ferguson, 1972), pp. 121-24.

[61]'Silvicultural History of Inverliever Forest', Forestry Commission typescript, n.d. (circa 1953). The major recommendation here to do with

species of trees best suited for the area (Silver Spruce) and with revising the optimistic estimates from early years concerning how large an area was suitable for planting.

[62]*Ford and District, op. cit.,* p. 26.

[63]'Silvicultural History', *op. cit.,* p.2.

[64]*Ibid.,* p. 4. The number of sheep declined from 6,500 in 1907 to 4.500 in 1953; the number of cattle increased from 30 to 35.

[65]Forestry Commission Annual Reports, 1920 through 1979; *Scottish Abstract of Statistics, 1981; Agricultural Statistics, Scotland,* 1919 through 1978. See Appendix for detailed figures.

[66]'Background Note on Inverliever Forest and the Village of Dalavich', prepared by Forestry Chief George Francey, 1981.

[67]Forestry Commission Reports; *Scottish Abstract of Statistics,* 1981. See Appendix for detailed figures.

[68]*Agricultural Statistics,* Scotland. For detailed figures, see Appendix.

[69]*Ibid.*

[70]Forestry Commission Reports. See Appendix.

[71]'Silvicultural History . . .' *op. cit.,* pp. 7-8.

[72]*The Third Statistical Account of Scotland, Argyll* (Glasgow: Collins, 1961), Appendix IV, p. 375.

[73]'Background Note on Inverliever Forest . . .' *op. cit.*

[74]*Ford and District, op. cit.,* pp. 30-31.

[75]*The Third Statistical Account of Scotland,* Vol. IX (The County of Argyll) (Glasgow: Collins, 1961), pp. 233-36.

[76]*Ford and District, op. cit.,* p. 21.

4 Ford Today:
the Structures of Social Life

*General character: The people are generally active,
humane, hospitable, middle-sized, and capable of
bearing cold, wet, and hunger to a great degree; they
are not given to drinking, though, from their social
disposition, when a number of them occasionally meet,
they are apt to take a sitting together.*
Statistical Account of Scotland
1794, Vol. 13, Glassary Parish.

Introduction

On the casual visitor today, Ford leaves the impression of
somnolence. When outsiders express this view, of course, it is
highly resented by the people of the village, first of all because it is
not true, and second because even if it were, it is not the place of
outsiders to say so. But the impression is there nonetheless,
summer and winter (though there is more traffic in summer).
Passers-through will not see people collected on the road except at
unusual times, they are not likely to encounter road jams, and they
do not linger long enough to penetrate the public surface of the
community to comprehend the social life that exists there. It is like
life in a tide-pool.

The quiet nature of community life is, in fact, a matter of pride
and enjoyment for most of the people, although the teenaged
population will voice their desires for more urban-oriented 'action'.
I was told by more than one person that villagers tire of hearing
from the summer tourists such remarks as 'How do you stand all
this peace and quiet?' and 'If it is this quiet in the summer, what on
earth do you do in the winter?' Indeed, Ford's native writer, the late

1 The village of Ford, 1983, viewed from near the burial island on Ederline Estate. (JBS)

2 Ford Post Office, painted by A. Scott Rankin for publication in Patrick Gillies' *Netherlorn, Argyllshire, and Its Neighbourhood*, published in 1909. (AC)

3 Ford Post Office as it appeared in 1983. (JBS)

4 Maimie Cameron, the Postmistress, one of seven native-born residents of Ford, and her husband, Dempster, retired gamekeeper for the Forestry Commission. (AC)

5 The village of Ford as it appeared on a postcard around 1910. (AC)

6 Ford, 1982. (AC)

7 Davie Murray pumping petrol for Alasdair Carmichael next to Ford Hotel, around 1970. The nearest petrol today is at Kilmartin, 3½ miles away. (AC)

8 David, Amy, and Ruaridh, with Davie Murray own and operate the Ford Hotel. (AC)

9 Alex MacDougall's wedding, 30 June 1932. Alex was born in 1895. The picture was taken on *Cnoc an Ath*, 'The Hillock at the Ford', an ancient burial mound next to the original ford and an old cattle stance. (AC)

10 Ford farmers and shepherds at a cattle sale in Oban, 1966. Although it has declined somewhat, hill-farming is still an important part of the village economy. (AC)

11 Members of t[

12 Members of the Ford Gun Club in 1980. (AC)

ub in 1880. (AC)

13 Alex MacDougall practising for an upcoming ploughing match with his Clydesdales at Creaganterve Farm in 1935. (He won.) With him is the late Archie Keith. (AC)

14 Ford Bay of Loch Awe. Once the site of the pier used by loch steamers putting into Ford, Ford Bay is now used mainly by anglers. (AC)

15 Cnoc an Ath, the burial mound across from the Ford Hotel. Unexcavated and unmarked, its significance is nonetheless known and respected by villagers. (JBS)

16 Tree-planting in Inverliever Forest, about 1964. Donald MacCallum, brother to the Postmistress, is on the left. Ronnie Mathieson and Robert Gillies are in the background. The Forestry Commission still provides work for a number of men in the village, as does private forestry. (AC)

17 Houses in 'The Row.' All but the rightmost house have been built since the late 1960s and are occupied by incomers. (JBS)

22 Schoolhouse at Ford, with the school attached at the rear. It has been used as a private residence since the school closed in the 1970s. (JBS)

23 Mr MacKinnon with sheep on Torran Mor Farm. (AC)

Alasdair Carmichael, took the trouble to write an answer to the last question in the form of a magazine article, because he had heard the question so many times.[1] (Among other things, he said wryly, the winter is spent picking up the litter left by the summer people.)

If the community called Ford is in fact more than the hotel, an occasional walk to the Loch, fishing, and a few glimpses of picturesque West Highland life, what is its substance, what are its structures, its patterns, its activities, and its own sense of being? What are the roles of family and kinship networks? How is work structured? What could be said about class and other divisions within the village? What kinds of organizations are there which structure community life? What are the focal points of village activity? Are there neighbourhood and friendship networks which are important to community life? How are services provided? What are the linkages to the economic and political spheres of which this small place is only a marginal part? And, in all of this, how does history interact with the present to produce the emergent social reality which is Ford?

Family and Kinship

There were 59 households in Ford in 1981. With a population of around one hundred and fifty occupying these households, it is only reasonable to surmise that family units are relatively small. This is indeed the case, although there are a few exceptions. Significantly, it would have to be said that kinship networks are not extensive in Ford; there are few instances of multiple-branch families living here under the same or different roofs, whether of the same or different generations. Unlike some rural communities where 'everyone is related to everyone else', the connections among the people of Ford are *not* primarily those of kinship. Relationships are not organized, for the most part, around one's relationship as a brother or sister, aunt or uncle, grandson or cousin to a set of other families in the village. Nor is it common for extended kin to remain under one roof, older parents tending to be provided separate housing here or in another village or town, for example.

The relative ease of transportation by car has made it possible for kinship ties to be maintained as social networks over a larger geographic area, so that there is visiting (overnight) by sisters, parents, brothers, etc. But there is not that daily interaction with extended kin which makes kinship the organizing principle of village life which it is in some communities.

Family relationships are important, of course, and they are kept up over long distances, but the fact of life is that most people in Ford have learned to live with that sense of distance, because the rate of out-migration continues to be high, taking members of the family to far-flung places such as Australia and Canada, as well as to closer communities such as Lochgilphead and Glasgow, and points between such as England.

The other major factor influencing the relative unimportance of kinship networks in the daily lives of villages is the nature of the in-migration to the community, which has brought in a quantity of couples whose children have grown and left home, and who have no kin either in the village or in the area. Those who do bring children with them, as many do, do not bring extended kin, and so even they cannot be said to contribute to a system of kinship networks.

Immediate family relationships of the kind shared with others under the same roof are very important in organizing the lives of Ford's people, as they are anywhere, and it is especially necessary to point this out after having said that kinship connections are weak or non-existent. The roles of parent, child, sibling, husband, wife, are highly significant ones here. Family members are nurturant and loyal. Family names are not unimportant. But there is no clannishness here and there are no clans, lest someone believe that the Highlands are still organized around clan ties. In the days when the families of Clan Campbell still held the lands around Ford, and when there was little mobility, the principles of societal organization were much different. But the clans have scattered, the lands have changed hands, and the presence of numerous incomers has made even the *idea* of clan and kin an anomaly today.

There is one aspect of so-called nuclear family relationships which deserves further mention. It is widely taken for granted that young people in the community have no future there. The young have been leaving the area since the beginning of the nineteenth century, and the tide of youthful population outflow has not stopped yet. Children know this, and their parents are only too well aware of it. The situation leads to a certain ambivalence in parent-child ties, and the dilemma becomes keener when the children enter their teen years. Parents and children are quite close, and families are very caring even if they rarely express their caring in public displays. And yet the children learn early that they will be independent, that they will live somewhere else in all likelihood, perhaps overseas. There is an inner sadness on the part of parents, and a feeling of loyalty and fondness for family and place on the part of the young. But the public statements reveal a resignation to the facts. A widowed mother says 'I have already learned to live alone.' A parent who has already seen one daughter leave says she cannot encourage her other children to stay here because 'There is nothing here for them.' A father says his son will definitely leave in a few years because 'There is no future for him here, and we both know that.'

Thus, there is probably a more pronounced shift in the parent-child relationship in the middle teen years, more noticeable than in places where large-scale migration is not so common—a change from nurturance to nurtured independence.Whatever sadness is associated with the recognition of the need for this preparation for independence is cushioned by the knowledge that it is not a new invention but the continuation of a pattern of long standing, accepted by everyone else as part of 'the way things are'.

Work

If multi-family kinship networks are not the key organizing principle in the village, there are others which orient the lives of the villagers. Work is important to most people in Ford, for example, even for some of those who have retired. 'Work' has, of course, come to mean mainly employment for monetary gain, but it still possesses some of the older, pre-cash-economy meaning of purposeful activity oriented to the accomplishment of tasks. Thus, while it is true that most people in Ford who work are employed for a wage or salary, or work for the income produced through trade and the provision of services, there are yet a very few families who involve family members in work for other than wages. The Ford Hotel, for example, although it employs a number of people from in and outside the village for its operation in the summer, could not function without the work of the whole family: David Murray, his wife Amy, his fifteen-year-old son Ruaridh, and the elder Mr Murray, now 77 (and sometimes even Amy's sister Kathy from nearby Lochgilphead). Likewise Duncan MacKinnon operates Torran Farm with little hired labour, depending on the children who remain at home to contribute their share—not to mention the help of Mrs MacKinnon. Work still incorporates maintaining a household and raising children, whether these duties are carried out by man, wife, or both, as in a few cases.

The shift to wage work, while it may not be complete, is in an advanced stage in Ford, so that we must look at what people do 'for a living' to understand how work organizes the lives of most Fordians.

For many people, work serves to bring them together. This is true of the employees of the Forestry Commission, who ride in a van to and from work together, and who often work as teams in the forest. The men who work in private forestry also work together. One newcomer to Ford, Joachim Brolly, employs two of his brothers, one of whom lives with him in Ford. Altogether he employs eight or nine men in timber work on Lochaweside, and they tend to work long hours as a team, remaining in radio contact even when they are separated. Among all those who work in the forests, whether for the Forestry Commission or for private contractors, there is at least the common bond of sharing the same kind of work.

Gamekeepers, too, share the same community of work despite the fact that, with the exception of those who work for the Forestry Commission as Rangers, none of them shares the same employer. Thus, Eddie MacLean, who is the keeper at Ederline, can discuss the fox problem with Dempster Cameron, retired Ranger, and the status of the deer population in neighbouring forests with Allen Booth, a self-employed deer stalker. When the Major invites friends for a November pheasant shoot, Eddie can call on a number of keeper friends and others to help with the beating, which requires fifteen to twenty men. (When the day's work is over, the beaters can repair to the pub for a dram or two and a laugh or two at the expense of the 'toffs' towards whose guns the men were driving the birds during the day.)

Work brings people together in other places, such as the hotel, where there may be eight people working in the dining room, kitchen, bar, reception area, rooms, and outside the building. The hotel is a major communications centre for the village, and considerable information sharing and opinion-shaping takes place among the people who work there as well as among the frequent visitors to the pub.

And work keeps together the families and other workers on the farms, such as Ederline, Auchinellan, and MacKinnon's. In short, there are many varieties of work which serve as nodular points of human contact in Ford, creating paths for individuals which cross the paths of others daily in patterned ways.

But it is not the case that work incorporates all of life for anyone (except perhaps Joachim Brolly and his brothers, who sometimes work 16-hour days and 7-day weeks in the forest), or that it always serves to pull people together. Increasingly, it would seem, the work that the people of Ford do takes them away from the village altogether, and for some of them it seems accurate to describe Ford as an occasional bedroom to which they return. One individual teaches daily in Lochgilphead, and another also commutes there daily for work as an adult education tutor and another works there for the District. One man's work as a geologist takes him to numerous places around the world for extended periods of time. Another man is at sea much of the time. Another works in Kilmichael. And so on. Home and work are increasingly separated for people in Ford, and, in fact, as we shall see later, it may be this fact which stabilizes or increases the population of the village, For not only is it possible to commute to work from Ford now, but there are places to which to commute.

Nevertheless, the kinds of work which draw people apart from the community, though they may be essential to the maintenance of numbers in the community, are a departure from traditional work forms which tend to draw people together.

Class and Other Divisions

In many communities, work operates as a dividing force among various categories of the population, primarily because work is class-linked—that is, people who work in different jobs associated with different prestige levels tend to choose people at their own prestige level with whom to associate rather than to cross job-related class lines. In the microcosm of Ford, personal esteem is more important than formal prestige (with an all-important exception which will be discussed). While it may be the case that some individuals with jobs which require more training associate less with those whose work places them on a lower scale in the wider society than the latter do with each other, the primary reason is the one just described—namely, the fact that the former commute out of the village to work and are not in Ford much of the time. Another cross-cutting factor is that many of the commuters are incomers only recently come to Ford, and many of those people (though not all by any means) have chosen, one presumes, not to enter into local associations to the degree that longer-term residents have.

Otherwise, class, considered in the sense of formal prestige associated with occupation and education, does not seem to play a large or direct role in defining community lines. In fact, there is in Ford, and in many other small communities in Scotland I am told, fairly strong pressure to ignore status, to play it down. The situation is reminiscent of Mathews' description of the 'so-so' ethic in a middle Tennessee community.[3] Both in Ford and in the Tennessee community there are subtle pressures which prevent individuals from 'getting above their raising' or lording it over anyone else, and at the same time there is help given or special circumstances cited when anyone happens to fall below an acceptable line. It is as though there were a large 'club' in Ford, and anyone who wants to belong is welcome. But being 'snooty' is frowned on, and it is very bad taste to show off or brag too much, or to take charge of a situation with too much authority. It is a club for equals, regardless of origins (exception to be noted) or achievements. There are some, particularly among the new incomers, who simply choose not to join because their time is spent elsewhere or their interests lie mainly outside the community.

(This story was told by a Lismore man to illustrate the jealousy which some here say is prevalent among Scots and which operates to prevent individuals from rising above the 'common level': An

Englishman, an Irishman, and a Scot were competing in a greasy pole contest. The Englishman's friends cheered him on, and had a large gin and tonic ready for him if he should win, but he could not make it to the top. The Irishman's friends backed his attempt with great fervour, even giving him a boost when the referee was not looking, but he could not make it either. When the Scotsman's turn came, he made it up the pole with no difficulty—but his friends came out and chopped down the pole.)

The most important class distinction in Ford is the same that would have been found (and was reported) in the area two hundred years ago: that between 'the gentry' and 'the other class', to quote an eighteenth century minister from Kilmartin. I could not say whether that line is any more or less uncrossable today than at any time in the past, but that the line is there is a clear and accepted fact. It seems to have nothing to do with personal qualities (esteem)— the laird can be described in the most glowing terms, even described as 'ordinary' and 'approachable', but he is still the laird. A good laird is one who spends enough time on his estate to know the land, the stock, the game, and especially the people who work for him, and he is one who is willing to spend the money needed to make necessary improvements on the land. He need not be exceedingly generous, but he must pay a living wage and a little extra sometimes, and he must not rub in his lairdly status, no matter how lowly the stature of the person in whose company he finds himself. But no matter if he is a bad laird and is the opposite of all these things, he is still the laird. One would not expect to be extended the same kind of hospitality and equal treatment that the laird would extend to his friends and acquaintances on his own level. He is not resented just because you are asked to work as a beater and are not invited to shoot with him (you will be invited to the beaters' shoot at the end of the season, and that is the courtesy you are due). You have your pint or a dram in the pub after the shoot and he has his drinks with his friends at his house, and each set of people has its own pleasures. The 'toffs', as the laird and his friends are called, seem neither to be envied nor resented, though the term seems to carry a tone of derision. One is no longer, as in former times, expected to tug at one's forelock or take off one's cap or otherwise show excessive deference, and I was told that one way in which the job of the gamekeeper has changed over the years is that one can use plain talk with the laird. The important thing now is to do one's job well.

But although the distinction between 'the gentry' and the 'other class' is still a strong one (even if not as commanding as in earlier times when lairds were richer and more powerful and the 'other class' more insolvent and without influence), it is relatively unimportant in Ford for all that. (I should add that in cases where the community is more an inclusive part of a single estate, this element of class structure would definitely be more important.) The reason for this is that the laird's life and the life of the rest of the village do not intrude upon each other at many crucial points.

There are, theoretically, two 'lairds' whose decisions and involvement could influence life in Ford. The 'laird' at Auchinellan is essentially a trust—the inheritor does not visit often, and she will not decide the fate of the estate for some years, when she becomes twenty years of age. The other is Major Warde-Aldam at Ederline. The kinds of decisions the Major makes in the management of Ederline are not of the sort that have much effect on the village, except that his employees represent five families in the village and he does hire casual labour from time to time. He and his wife are sometimes involved in community affairs, but not often—they do not play leadership roles, at least of a visible nature. The people of Ford always know when they are in residence, but theirs is not an intrusive presence. They are well respected by villagers, and they in turn respect and show concern for the people of Ford. It is an accepted and harmonious relationship, but the Warde-Aldams, probably because they are gentry, are somewhat removed from the daily structure of life in the village. Their role in the large scheme of things is a key one, as would be anyone's who owned 13,000 acres of the neighbourhood and provided a means of livelihood for five families. This key role would become prominent only when large-scale decisions about the estate might be made—if the estate were sold, for example, or if the Major were to give up farming and convert the estate to forest plantation entirely (neither of which options is being remotely considered to my knowledge)—but otherwise the power of the laird is not felt even though its presence is tacitly acknowledged.

Although, with the exception just noted, there seem to be no strong class lines in the village, there are other types of non-class division. One, which will be taken up in a later section, is the distinction between long-term residents and incomers. This is a complex division and requires detailed discussion. The term 'incomer' is sometimes confounded with being English, and it also is difficult to know exactly how long one's residence needs to be before one is no longer new to the community, but the point is that the category of newcomer is recognized and has a high, if somewhat variable membership.

There is also a division between those who are faithful attenders of church and those who never go, but this is not a major division of the community either in terms of numbers or the importance attached to it by most villagers. Church is held twice a month in Ford Church of Scotland and involves from twelve to fifteen worshippers, or about ten percent of the village. Most are older persons (in their fifties to their eighties), a somewhat larger number are female than male, and the proportion who have recently settled in the village is small—though the incomers who do participate are important to the church. This division is one which seems to be understood and accepted widely—it has no doubt been present many decades and centuries, and it is not unique to the West Highlands of Scotland. It is similar in some respects to the division between 'saints' and 'sinners' found in fundamentalist churches in Appalachia: if you drink, for example, you don't go to church, and if you go to church, you don't drink. The Church of Scotland is described as too 'Calvinist' by some of the English incomers who are more accustomed to the greater liberalism of Church of England doctrines. Many of the native Scots in the village find the church a bit too exclusive, saying, 'I think you will find more Christians outside than inside the church here.' But in general, the distinction between churchgoer and non-churchgoer is not fore-most in the minds of the people on either side of it. It is not sufficient to separate people from each other in and of itself, though it may define certain places and times when one group will not be in the company of the other. (When my family and I attended church in Ford in November, I noted that there was only one present, excluding ourselves, who had been in the pub the night before).

The Church

We cannot know how central the church has been in village life during its history; perhaps it was once very strong in its membership and in the extent to which it influenced the affairs of the community or its families. The Church of Scotland has not been the only church here; there was a Free Kirk at Creaganterve for a time, and there was a Free Kirk in Ford near the Post Office, although neither has survived to the present. But if religious zeal and church activism were high at some time in the past, they are not high now. The church was built of sturdy material in 1848 to seat over one hundred worshippers, but it is eighty to ninety percent empty on preaching days now.

The building is attractive, built of native stone along simple architectural lines in accordance with plans drawn up by the resident architect at Poltalloch Estate. In the late nineteenth century, Henry Bruce of Ederline had stained glass windows installed in memory of members of his family, and when worshippers gaze upon the figures representing Faith, Hope and Charity, they are reminded that Mrs Bruce's bones lie under the cross on the burial island at Ederline. An old pump organ, improved by an electric motor, huffs away at time-honoured Scottish hymn tunes under the capable hands of Miss Greenshields. An occasional visitor might pick up what appears to be the New Testament and be mystified by the unfamiliar Gaelic, for there are still one or two copies to be found in the pew-racks. It is a place of charm and warmth (at least twice a month when the heat is turned on), but it is not used much. 'People will want to use it for weddings,' I was told, 'but then they don't come to church. They just want the church *there*, if you know what I mean, but they don't support it themselves.' But the fact is that there are not many weddings in Ford, and wanting the use of the church seems a remote issue. The only wedding which took place during my visits to Ford brought together Robert Gillies of Ford and his bride from Slockavullin in a ceremony performed in Kilmartin church.

It may nonetheless be true that people in the village want a church there, whether they use it or not, because it simply would not be a 'complete' village without it. When the primary school closed in 1972, it was a considerable blow to the entire village. When the teacher, Miss Mathiesson, organized village meetings and called in local education authorities to hear the lamentations of the community, many attended who did not have, and never had had children in the school, because they feared the loss of what they thought was a vital institution. I think much the same reasoning goes on today concerning the church: a church is part of the standard furniture of any village with substance, and the loss of the church simply makes the village of Ford that much more insubstantial. Thus, for most of the village, the problem, insofar as it is one, has little to do with theology or the realization of the various worthy missions of the church. For the churchgoers, of course, the threatened loss of the church means something else.

Indeed, there are some in Ford who, with justification, feel that a decision may soon be made to close their church. The man who was minister in 1981, Revd Arthur Law, who also served three other small churches in this and the neighbouring parish, looked at the future rather statistically. The future of the church will depend on the population situation, he said, and unfortunately, the population in the area is diminishing. In 1945-46 Kilmartin had over 230 on the communion roll. Now there are about 50 or 60. 'Unless something appears out of the blue, I can't imagine it increasing.' The congregations at the other two churches—Kilmichael and Lochgair—are larger. Ford is a 'mission station' of Kilmartin. And because the Ancient Monuments office is interested in Kilmartin Church—on account of the ancient stones in the churchyard and the cross inside the church—this interest may afford it some unique protection, according to Revd Law.

The church faithfuls are aware of the vulnerability of Ford Church of Scotland. They have seen the church enjoy better times and they can imagine worse ahead. Says Mrs McNair: 'There are no more Gaelic services, which used to be held at 12.00 noon, followed by English services at 1.00 p.m. What has happened to the church? People are just not being brought up in it. They want the church there, but they leave it to the few to carry it on. I don't know what will happen to the church after we in the older generation pass away.'

But though the people may blame themselves or each other for the atrophy which seems to have set in, the church itself should bear some of the responsibility—the church in this case being the larger church bodies reponsible for local parish churches. For it was someone at a higher level who years ago made a decision in the name of efficiency to consolidate these four small congregations into one call, creating an almost impossible situation for the most dedicated and long-legged minister. It is little wonder that both churchgoers and non-churchgoers complain that the minister doesn't visit as in the old days, or that 'We don't see the minister hardly at all here.' It is simply impossible for one person to cover the territory and become involved in communities to the extent that he should. Consequently, ministers cannot understand the nature of local community concerns and help local people respond to them; nor can they possibly minister to the needs of all the individuals in the four churches, or meet newcomers and draw them into church activities. The minister's reponsibilities are so organized (or disorganized) that he cannot provide vital spiritual or community leadership to places like Ford, with the consequence that the vitality of the local church is reduced. It is at least a contributing factor which needs consideration alongside the influence of population change.

One hundred and thirty years after its birth, the church in Ford faces the most critical time of its existence. If it should die, it would be sorely missed by a few and would be a source of nostalgia for others. If it were to become reinvigorated, it might become a vital, inclusive community institution. At present, it is not.

Other Formal Organizations

Community life in Ford is structured by more than the church, obviously. Among the various formalized groups and activities deserving mention are the Village Hall (within that broad category of programmes and activities there are a number of long- and short-term organizations), the Ford SWRI and the Ford Gun Club.

The Village Hall was built in 1968. Many of the activities which might once have taken place in the school, which closed in 1972, take place there. The construction and furnishing of the Hall are matters of pride for the many who took part—everyone enjoys telling how it came about. A committee was organized; it approached the County Council and secured a grant for the building. For a period of several years, virtually everyone in the village, young and old, male and female, helped with fund-raising by organizing and participating in sales of work, whist drives, dances, and similar activities. Newcomers and old-timers were rewarded by the sight of the tangible result of their joint efforts, and by the good parties they staged to pay for it. It was paid off very quickly and it became the focal point for numerous programmes and gatherings which for several years occupied the building almost every night of the week.

In addition to the occasional ceilidh, the Hall was used by a newly organized youth club which became very popular among village children (there were 13 of them between the ages of 5 and 12). It became the meeting site for 'the Rural', the Scottish Women's Rural Institute of Ford, for its monthly meetings. Scottish country dances were held once or twice a week. Whist drives and sales of work took place monthly to benefit the Hall or the programmes which took place in it. A 'Keep Fit Club' was begun in the Hall for about ten women in the village. An unsuccessful attempt was made to start an old people's club and a well-baby clinic. And two badminton clubs, one for youth and one for adults were begun.

The initiative came not only from the long-term residents like David Murray, but from recent incomers (of the time) like the MacNays, who eagerly brought in new ideas about worthwhile community organizations. Such ideas, together with the practical planning, oversight, and bookkeeping required to keep the Village Hall going, were and are carried out by the Village Hall Committee, which has always had members from among the newer as well as the older residents of Ford. The Hall Committee is a microcosm of the village itself, displaying in miniature the harmonies and tensions which exist among elements of the community. In working out policies and practical decisions regarding the Hall, it governs the use of one of the important focal points of social life in Ford.

The Hall Committee itself is small (six people), but the number of people involved in the various uses of it is quite large even today, when it is used less frequently than when it was new. While it cannot be said that everyone in the community is involved in one or another Hall-related activity, still every sector of the village is represented at one time or the other (with the exception of the Major and his family).

The Hall is still the site of SWRI meetings, and whist drives and sales of work still involve twenty or thirty people each month. The badminton clubs remain active after 13 years. A new pre-school play group has started up this year for eight children of the mothers involved in it. And a Christmas party (an annual event) is being planned. But for all that, the Hall is not used as frequently as when it was new. There are no more Scottish country dances and very few ceilidhs. The youth club has ceased to function. The Keep Fit Club no longer meets.

Why this decrease in activity? One theory offered by a family in the village is that there is no reservoir of leadership, and that when those who are actively involved tire and wish to step aside, there is no one there to take their places. Another person explained that the youth group ceased about five years ago mainly because there was a gap in the ages of children in the village, and the numbers simply were not there to carry the programme forward.

The dances, according to one notion, disappeared as the bands became more loud and more expensive. But a major contributing factor in ending the dances and the ceilidhs was the legislative change made in the closing hours of bars across the entire country. In accordance with the Licensing Act (Scotland) 1976, allowable bar closing hours were extended from 10.00 to 11.00 p.m., and as the Murrays explain the consequence, the new bar hours spelled the death of other forms of social activity. Before the 11.00 o'clock closing, people might gather in the pub, enjoy a few refreshments, and then decide shortly after 9.00 to have a gathering in the Hall, to which they would then adjourn for an impromptu ceilidh. Now, with the closing at 11.00, the hour is too late, people are tired and ready for bed or too full of refreshment to care.

Another factor which may have contributed to the decline of the village parties in the Hall is the changing mix of the population. A number of individuals who would have made important contributions to dancing and ceilidhs, for example, are no longer 'in life'. Alasdair Carmichael is one such individual. He knew not only local history and lore, he had Gaelic and was an accomplished story-teller and Scottish dancer. As people like Alasdair passed from the scene in the time since the Hall was completed less than fifteen years ago, numerous others have moved into the village from England and urban Scotland, people who, even if they had an appreciation for things Scottish, which some of them do, can only enjoy local culture and not contribute to it in traditional ways.

Last, these forms of village entertainment have been displaced by the passive absorption of Ford's people into the world of television, which came to Ford when the community's cable antenna was erected by a village committee in 1977.

Still, although the kinds of activities have changed in certain respects and the sheer amount of activity may be less these days than ten years ago, the Village Hall is very important to the community and the Hall Committee serves as a rotating, representative guiding body which attempts to keep it alive and vital.

Another organization which deserves mention is the Scottish Women's Rural Institute, whose branch in Ford includes about 15 members. 'The Rural' is quite an old organization nationally (there are a Canadian and an English as well as a Scottish version), with its headquarters in Edinburgh. I cannot think of a close counterpart organization in the United States unless it might be the federally sponsored Home Demonstration Clubs. The Rural is a private concern which provides a broad range of educational, personal improvement, and community improvement programmes for its members, relying to a considerable extent on the initiative of local members to carry out the programmes that are planned and/or offered centrally. This outreach programme has involved thousands of women over the years in numerous projects of civic and family importance, and it has been an important means for rural women to become connected to each other in purposeful shared activity. As mentioned earlier, one of the most important products of the Ford group was the *Ford and District* history compiled by the members as part of a national competition in 1966. The Rural in Ford meets monthly, and takes up topics of mutual interest such as foreign travel, handwork, and floral art.

The Ford Gun Club is a remarkable organization if for no other reason than its longevity, for surely there are few such villages with such a fluctuating population which can claim clubs over one hundred years old. No doubt the organization grew out of the shared interest of the concentration of gamekeepers and sportsmen which grew in the Ford area during the latter half of the nineteenth century when so many of the estates were converted to sport. A calendar of shoots is still maintained each year, involving not only the men of Ford (and it is exclusively male), but men from neighbouring villages such as Eredine. A typical shoot held in October, 1981, included 65 guns. 'Friendly' matches are held as well as competitive matches between village teams. David Murray and Hamish MacNeill are largely responsible for organizing the shoots for the Ford club. It provides an important seasonal coming-together for many of the men of the area and is for them perhaps the counterpart of the estate-sponsored shootings for the toffs.

The inventory of formal organizations in the village thus includes:

The Church of Scotland

The Village Hall and its various programmes and activities, including:
The Junior and Senior Badminton Clubs
The Play Groups
The whist drives and sales of work for the benefit of the Hall and its programmes
Occasional discos for the teenagers

The Ford SWRI

The Ford Gun Club

Informal Ties, Friends and Neighbours, and the Pub

Informal types of networks are at least equally as important as the formal ones in the structure of the social life in Ford. The role of family and kinship has already been discussed, as has the importance of associations (usually of men) based on work. The other focal points of social life in the village deserve attention: the hotel pub, and friendships.

The centrality of the pub to the community must be experienced to be fully appreciated. Only as one spends time there does one begin to recognize that it is much more important than the church, the Post Office, the grocery shop, the telephone, or at-home visits among friends as the way in which friendships are maintained, information exchanged, advice solicited and given, and group activity enjoyed among a wide spectrum (although not all) of the community. On Friday and Saturday nights particularly, and even more particularly when the summer season has ended and the tourists are gone, the pub is a scene of intense sociability. (The hotel closes to overnight guests in October—except for the stray visiting professor—and the small dining tables in the bar are removed to make way for the snooker table. The dart board, which has been there all along, is illuminated, and the electronic scorer comes to life. The *bar*, which serves the touring public throughout the summer months, is recaptured by the local people in October and converted instantly and magically into the *pub*.)

More people by far gather at the pub on these evenings than anywhere else at any time in Ford. More men than women are there, but social conventions have changed and it is not at all uncommon for women to be there with or without male accompaniment. Only the churchgoers, the elderly, the non-drinkers, and many of the recent incomers are not there. Pub people come in from Eredine and Dalavich and Kilmartin as well as Ford. They stand at the bar and talk and buy drams of whisky and pints of beer for each other, or they play darts and talk, or they play snooker and talk. The deerstalker meets the gamekeeper and their wives meet and talk, and the gamekeeper talks to the son of the nurseryman, who has brought the daughter of a timber contractor with him. The timber man is playing darts with his wife and a Forestry Commission Ranger and a shopkeeper, and they all talk to the mother and daughter-in-law of another timber worker, who is standing at the bar with a fellow worker and a member of the hotel dart team who speaks to a couple who recently retired and moved to Ford. And on it goes until it reaches full circle, the chain unbroken among forty or fifty men and women, young and old, the barman and his wife and father and the visiting professor and his wife and son caught up in the middle of the warm companionship, all fighting their knowledge of the cold, bitter rain outside. The whole world, for a moment, is in here.

There are quieter times as well, when people discuss the events of the day, or trade new gossip and the old stories of the village, catch up on illnesses, problems and successes, make plans for new ventures, seek advice or information, or try to recapture former times. Almost everything gets discussed here: the agenda of the Hall Committee; who has returned from holiday; the progress of home improvement projects; the departure of Revd Law for Blair Drummond; the frustrations of child-rearing; the loss of hens to foxes; sheep prices; Scotland's footballing chances in the World Cup next year, and dart league competitions. It is not the place, however, for airing personal problems or family disputes—the barman is not supposed to be the counsellor or psychoanalyst for his patrons. (In fact, Scots—Britons in general—do not discuss their problems as freely as Americans. They are not given to revealing themselves easily if it might show a flaw or defect. I asked one man in the pub why he had moved from Ford to Eredine. He sized up the situation momentarily, smiling pleasantly, deciding how much he needed to tell me. A third person was present, listening—someone who knew the answer. 'Simple,' he said. 'Marital problems and financial difficulties.' He laughed it off. I could imagine a similar situation in the States where with an opening such as that a man in a bar would spend the remainder of the night pouring out his woes to an unfortunate listener, but from the man in Ford all I got was the undecorated truth in five words.)

The hotel pub is the place where one will find announcements about the activities of the Ford Gun Club and the Ford darts team. (There is a glass-enclosed bulletin board across the road near the church which also carries news of whist drives, discos at Dalavich, and meetings of various kinds.) It is not the only communication centre in the village—people stop at the Post Office to find out things from Maimie Cameron, or they stop in at McLain's grocery shop or Mrs Ross's Craft Shop—but the pub is the main switch-board.

The hotel is especially busy on nights when darts matches are staged there. The Ford team, which includes some from Eredine as well as Ford, is sponsored by the hotel, which means that the pub at Ford is their home ground. There are eight people to a team (always, or almost always men), and when two teams are in the same pub with their friends, girl-friends, wives, and fans along, it is bound to make for a rowdy evening. But for all the noise and racket, there is seldom any unpleasantness—no fights or strong words. Losers buy a round for winners, and one may suppose that this gesture is sometimes a grudging one, but that is as tense as it gets.

Darts in Scotland is not a children's game. It is very serious business, with teams organized into leagues and important national matches played on television for high stakes. There are companies which specialize in outfitting and equipping darts playing areas, and the players all have their own personal darts which they carry in cases. (The plastic flights on one player's darts are adorned with the very Scottish red lion rampant on a yellow ground; another set has American flags.) Matches are held once a week somewhere in the area, which means that in the winter these men and their families (if any) organize their lives around serious darts and the pubs at least once every seven days. The men are good friends. They grow that special bond which is peculiar to groups that win and lose together. The darts team is thus another kind of structure which directs and shapes parts of people's lives in Ford, a structure which in this case is part of the hotel's pub life and which sometimes overlaps with work groups

I mentioned earlier that although the pub is the most central focus of social life in Ford, it does not encompass the entire community (in fact, no social organization is totally encompassing of everyone in a community, even in a small village like Ford). Pubs do not exclude. They have no admissions rules except for age and hours. It is not in their best interests to be known for exclusion. Rather, some people in Ford choose not to frequent the pub for any of several reasons. They may not be friendly with the people they are likely to find there; or they may be non-drinkers who do not enjoy being in the company of drinkers; or they may feel that a pub is an inappropriate place for someone such as themselves; or they may feel that the whole idea of the pub is wasteful of human energy and money; or they may feel that it promotes sin. For one or another of these reasons one will not find steady churchgoers in the pub, nor many elderly persons, nor many people who have recently moved into Ford. (A major exception to the last named rule is the Alstons, who drop into the pub almost every evening just before closing. Tommy Alston, originally from Glasgow, retired and moved to Ford a little over a year ago after working in Yorkshire for many years.) But even with the exceptions and exclusions, the pub is more inclusive of the community than any other single community organization or activity. It is the biggest 'club' in town.

It is a club with a peculiarly Scottish flavour, which may explain why it is not totally inclusive of the village. Likely as not when you come in the door you will hear Scottish dance band music from the tape player behind the bar. You will hear distinctively Scottish accents, and the people will be named McVean, McIntyre, McCuig, McLean, and McNeill. (It is not really so simple as this, however: there are also Scots in the pub named Beaton, Smith, and Alston, and there is one English couple—never in the pub—named MacNay.) And most of the time you find behind the bar one Davie Murray, David's father, who wears the Murray tartan kilt each and every day because, he says, he doesn't own a pair of trousers. He is the perfect Scottish Highland host, with a cheery greeting for everyone, and a good story told in a most charming broad Scots tongue. The whole atmosphere of the place is *Scottish* rather than *British*, and it is possible that some of the English do not feel entirely at home there.

The pub also seems to be more inclusive of those whose work is in Ford or very close at hand than of those who are 'commuters' to places like Lochgilphead. The commuters may represent the beginnings of a new class in Ford, although no such hard category exists in the minds of people there now. They are people whose work takes them outside, people whose orientations are turned as much outside as inwards toward Ford, people who, in some cases at least, use Ford as a place to park their families while they go to work, and park themselves overnight. Once again, this is a generalization subject to the usual exceptions, such as the incomer Brian Johns: Brian works in Lochgilphead as an architect but is active in the Ford Gun Club, and his wife took the lead in organizing the new village play group for pre-school children, of which they have two.

One additional network of human relationships in the village requires mention, and that is friendships, for friendships (and their opposite number, animosities) play an observable role in structuring and shaping village life. It is not necessary to discuss in detail who is friends with whom; a few generalities will suffice to make the point. Work brings friends together as in the case of the men who work together in forestry. Neighbouring people tend to become friends, as in the case of people who occupy the eight flats at Torran Mor, or some of the people who live in 'The Row'. Church, school, Village Hall activities, and pub social life all tend to create and enhance friendships. The friendships are important not only for the personal nourishment and support they provide the partners in the relationships, but also because of the networks of communication and practical help that exists because of them. As Ruby Campbell, single and in her sixties, says about life in the flats at Torran, 'The people at Torran have been wonderful. We help each other. It's just a wee community in itself.' Other residents at Torran run little errands for Ruby, who does not drive. Ruby watches after some of the small children when the mothers need to be away.

Friendships are important, but not everyone is friendly, of course. Most people are friendly because, as one man said 'We have to be. This is a small place.' But there are a few who just have nothing to do with each other and two families who do not speak to each other. The friendships seem frequently to cross potential dividing lines in the village, e.g., church and non-church, or recent incomer and long-time resident, which shows that the dividing lines are not rigid, even though perhaps the somewhat more typical pattern is for the friendships to remain within the lines. The one rare case of strong animosity is, perhaps significantly, between a Scottish incomer from 23 years ago and a more recent incomer couple who arrived in Ford 13 years ago. This relationship, which has been generalized by some other village people into an alleged pattern of antagonism between all long-term, native Scottish residents and recent incoming English 'white settlers', is both more and less than it appears to be. It is more because more has been made of it; it is less because it is the only instance of its extreme type. More will be said of this later.

My impression is that in Ford, friendship networks play much the same role that kinship networks would have played if they were stronger here, at least in the sense that they provide systems of borrowing, help, exchange, support, and nurturance. They keep people in communication and offer opportunities for confiding. They provide role-sets and patterned expectations, to lapse into the jargon, and thus give meaning, purpose, and structure to lives.

Ties to Larger Structures

The intersecting networks of human relationships in Ford need to be understood in order to comprehend the ways in which village life is patterned. But understanding the friendships and divisions, the organizations and focal points of interaction, the diminished role of kinship and of the church, is not enough to explain how life in Ford is maintained from day to day and year to year. Ford, although it may seem isolated to some, is not self-sufficient. The fact that electricity only came in 1963, television in 1977, and piped water in 1964, and that it is located at the intersection of one-track roads with passing places, should not fool anyone. It has not been cut off from the rest of Scotland or the world for centuries, if it ever was. After all, Ford came into being because it lay on an important transportation route.

If the minister at Kilmartin wrote in 1794 that everyone living in the parish was from that area with the exception of two shepherds, it was none-the-less true that the gentry and their factors and tacksmen (the middlemen) travelled extensively and sometimes even lived outside the country. Ordinary farmers stayed in touch with people outside the parish when they took their cattle to market. And service in numberless armed conflicts took men and boys from the area regularly to fight in far-off lands. The farms and estates were part of an entrenched system of rights and ownership that meant they often felt the consequences of decisions made in distant cities by men and women whose interests were anything but oriented to such marginal localities as Highland Scotland. The nature of the connections between places like Ford and larger economic and political systems has shifted and tightened from time to time over the decades, but it cannot be doubted that the connections were always there.

What are those connections today? What is the relationship between Ford and these larger systems? Put very simply, it is one of dependence. This point is clear, first, from an examination of ways in which basic services are provided. There is no doctor in Ford as there was in the early nineteenth century; the nearest is now in Lochgilphead. Nursing service is provided by nurses who travel into Ford from outside. As mentioned, there is no longer a school in Ford; beginning in 1938 the older children were sent to Oban and Lochgilphead to high school, and later the younger ones were sent by van to Kilmartin. The fragile dependence of the church has already been discussed. Some food is produced locally in gardens, but much more food is brought in than is produced locally. Because home-killing is illegal, little of the mutton, lamb or beef on the hills finds its way directly to local tables. Mobile grocers used to come to Ford, but improved transportation has meant that more people drive to nearby towns for shopping (twice-weekly bus service is available to Lochgilphead for those who cannot arrange car travel). Gas and coal delivered from Lochgilphead and Dalmally have replaced the locally-produced peat and wood fuels. A mobile bank rolls into Ford every Wednesday at noon. The mobile library has replaced the county library's branch in the village school.

Another aspect of the dependence of the locality on larger systems can be seen in the systems of subsidies by which hill farming is maintained. Everyone involved in farming in the area concurs that agriculture is not economically feasible here. Farmers may expect to break even, or to enjoy a profit of one percent or two percent per year at most, only because they receive subsidies. And the subsidies come not only from the government of the United Kingdom; since Britain joined the EEC (Common Market), the most important subsidies come from that international governmental agency. Because the Highlands are included in the EEC's 'Less Favoured Regions' category, the hill farmers of Argyll receive larger subsidies than they would otherwise. The systems of subsidies were implemented mainly for two reasons: to keep people on the land and thereby help stem the tide of rural depopulation, and to keep food prices as low as possible for the consumer. Without government payments for sheep and cattle raised in Ford, the farmers could not afford to farm, and there is little doubt that they would have to leave the land. The estates would also have to be turned to other purposes.

Estates such as Ederline and Auchinellan, as already pointed out, have always been dependent on money from outside for their upkeep. Until about the second third of this century, they were dependent essentially on 'private subsidies', that is, money that the lairds made elsewhere and put to work on the estates. But in more recent times, because of changes in government policies, they have benefited from public subsidies just as the smallholders have. What keeps Ederline home farm going, for example, is a combination of income from sales of stock raised there, EEC and UK subsidies, and, when it is needed, the profits the Major makes from his more solvent dairy enterprise in Yorkshire. The fact of the dependence of the estates is not new, but the form of it is.

Connections to larger systems are also starkly clear in the other economic sectors of Ford, such as forestry and tourism. Employment in the Forestry Commission, which was seen as a blessing in perpetuity by many observers decades ago, has shrunk and will probably continue to shrink as a result of forces quite outside the control of local people: mechanization, market fluctuations, and government policy regarding forestry (and other parts of the economy relating to forestry, such as fuel costs, lending rates, and public support for wood-using industries). Much the same can be said about the private timber businesses operating in Ford. The pulpwood market was seriously threatened by the recent closure of the giant Wiggins Teape pulp mill near Fort William, and was saved only by quick action which makes large new exports possible (although this solution produced some absurdities of its own: most pulpwood is now exported to Scandinavian countries which produce pulp to sell back to the United Kingdom for processing into paper.) The international wood market is like a delicate drama which can only be watched by hapless but hopeful people like those in Ford whose jobs depend on how it unfolds.

The community is likewise dependent on outside forces for the flow of tourists through it. How many people come through Ford, how many stay, how long they stay, and how much money they bring with them depend, for example, on the general state of the world's economies and how much spendable income people have.

Rising unemployment (almost three million are unemployed out of Britain's total population of around 42 million, and there are parts of Glasgow with unemployment as high as 30 percent) and escalating inflation have taken their toll on the tourist industry in United Kingdom. Rising petrol prices (the price in the autumn of 1981 was about $3.40 per imperial gallon) have also threatened the tourist trade, especially in the outlying areas of Scotland.

The Highlands have sought help from the British government for so long that reference to 'the Highland Problem' is even more firmly established as part of the government vocabulary than 'the Appalachian Problem' is in the United States. The latest form of assistance in solving Highland development problems is the Highlands and Islands Development Board, established in 1965 with a strong mandate to promote economic development, improve local infrastructures, and protect the unique features of Highland culture. Critics of the HIDB point out that whatever benefits and improvements can be shown in employment and raised standards of living in the region in the past 15 years can be attributed to events which would have taken place without it, such as the North Sea oil developments, but the fact is that the HIDB has encouraged numerous projects, some large and most small, which would not have been attempted otherwise. Ford, for example, has benefited from the HIDB's largesse, which helped with the construction of the cable television antenna in 1974, and helped launch a new fish farm at Ford (which, unfortunately, was not successful). When there are new ideas now for enterprise development in Ford, the people know they can contact their HIDB field representative 12 miles away in Lochgilphead for advice and, perhaps eventually, the capital to get started in business. This is one additional way in which Ford is tied into larger economic systems at regional, national and international levels.

The very composition of the population in Ford seems dependent on forces and factors which operate in contexts far removed from this locality. The nature of the community, its character and makeup, are changing as the roads to Ford take some people away and bring new ones in. How this is happening and with what consequences are subjects deserving more extensive treatment.

Footnotes

[1]Alasdair Carmichael, 'When the Visitors are Gone', *Scots Magazine* (January 1974), pp. 412-418.

[2]Kinship networks were also missing from a Scottish border village studied in the 1950s, according to James Littlejohn's *Westrigg, The Sociology of a Cheviot Parish* (London: Routledge and Kegan Paul, 1963), pp. 5ff.

[3]Elmora Messer Mathews, *Neighbor and Kin, Life in a Tennessee Ridge Community* (Nashville: Vanderbilt University Press, 1965).

5 Ford Today:
Depopulation and Repopulation

Everyone who now lives in Ford is an
incomer, although some have lived
here for thirty years. You'll not
find a native any older than I.
A Ford Resident, age 45

A glance at the population table for Kilmartin parish (see Table 5-1) tells the story. Only about a fifth the number of people are living here that were here 150 years ago. Historical records show that over two hundred years ago when fighting men were called out, great numbers issued forth from what are now deserted glens. The Census for 1841 shows 31 people from age 4 to 73—McPhails, McDouglas, McKellars, Campbells, McDonalds, Patersons, McNeils, Blues, McEustons, Sinclairs, and McKays—living in Ford just on the one farm of Torranbeg. Indeed, until the turn of the century, according to a burial stone at Kilineuair Church, one family was in residence at Torranbeg over generations spanning 500 years. Now Torranbeg consists of one house with one occupant.

The extent of population loss in the West Highland Region over the hundred years previous to Fraser Darling's *West Highland Survey* is rather staggering. He estimated that the total net outward migration for the hundred years up to 1955 amounted to well over 150,000—'considerably more than the entire population at the present time'.[1] He points out that emigration losses were partially offset by small natural increases up until about 1900, but that since then because of declining birth rates in most sections of the West Highlands, including the area of Kilmartin Parish, a small rate of natural decrease was overcome by the effects of emigration to bring

107

about continued depopulation. While this trend was taking its toll of the Highland population, the rest of Scotland was gaining in numbers, absorbing part of the drainage of people from the Highlands.

Table 5-1
Population of Kilmartin Parish, 1755-1971

Year	Population
1755[a]	1,150
1801	1,501
1811	1,453
1821	1,452
1831	1,475
1841	1,233
1851	1,144
1861	949
1871	869
1881	811
1891	695
1901	663
1911	582
1921	557
1931	455
1941	—
1951	460
1961	370
1971	326
1981	371

Webster's report in 1755 lists no 'Papists' in 'Kilmartine' parish, and states that out of the 1,150 persons living there, 230 are fighting men, that is, men between the ages of 18 and 50. He rejects the definition of 'fighting men' as those between 16 and 60, 'the one being generally too weak to bear the fatigues of War and the weight of Arms; and the other too Crazy and Infirm . . .'

Sources: James Gray, *Scottish Population Statistics, Including Web-ster's Analysis of Population, 1755* (Edinburgh: T. and A. Constable, 1962); F. Fraser Darling, *West Highland Survey* (Oxford: University Press, 1955); *Census of Population, Scotland*.

Darling assumed, or hoped, perhaps, that the population was beginning to stabilize near the 1951 figures, but he was incorrect in at least the case of Kilmartin parish, where the numbers fell for at least another two decades, from 460 persons in 1951 to 370 in 1961, and to 326 in 1971 (see Table 5-1). For the Highlands and Islands as a whole, data presented by Bryden and Houston show that there was a slight rise in population between 1951 and 1971, from 278,000 to 282,966.[2] But all this increase was experienced by urban areas and large and small burghs. From 1961 to 1971, they report the rural population fell by around 4,000. (The increases were realized mainly in Inverness and in Ross and Cromarty around the Moray and Cromarty Firths as well as other sites affected by North Sea oil developments, and at Fort William where the giant pulp mill and a neighbouring paper mill had been opened in the nineteen-sixties.)[3]

1981 Census figures for Scotland as a whole and its constituent governmental regions reveal that while the country dropped in population from 5,229,000 in 1971 to 5,117,000 (a decrease of 2.1 percent), the Highland Region increased from 175,000 in 1971 to 200,000 (an increase of 14.3 percent).[4] For the country as a whole, net migration fell in 1981, as did the birth rate and (consequently) the rate of natural increase. It is likely that the increase of population experienced in the Highland Region is attributable to increased inmigration coupled with a decrease in outmigration; the rate of natural increase is not likely to have been sufficient to explain the shift.

The explanation for the change in migration pattern is probably the attraction of employment prospects connected with oil develop-ments; the trend has only recently been identified and deserves further study. Again, according to the Census figures, the population of Argyll and Bute District increased between 1971 and 1981, from 65,000 to almost 68,000 (about 5 percent). For the first time since the Census of 1801, moreover, the population of Kilmartin

Parish increased from 326 in 1971 to 371 in 1981 (about 14 percent).

In Ford itself, the 170-year pattern of loss due to net migration (and even possibly to natural decrease as birth rates fell and death rates rose), also seems to have turned a corner, judging from local unofficial counts. The number of people counted in Ford by the SWRI for the local history was 109.[5] My count, in November 1981 was 156. The direction of difference in these numbers, even if they are not perfectly accurate, is consistent with the everyday observations of longer-term residents of the village. I was told, for example, on my first visit to Ford, that 'The population has been going down here for many years, but recently it has gone back up again, maybe to as many as 140 or 150, because of incomers, mainly from the south.'

But for over a century and a half, depopulation has been the master trend in Ford, Argyll, and the Highlands generally. Although the Statistical Accounts of Scotland make clear the fact of this depopulation, they appear cautious in their interpretations and explanations of it, attributing it to such causes as emigration to America and the drift of men southwards to Glasgow and England in search of work. These 'causes' are still operating today. But what lies behind them? Large-scale outmigration is more often than not a human adaptation to a problem situation—a push—coupled with the pull of perceived advantages of life in the area of destination. What were the push factors in Argyll and the Highlands which drove families to seek advantage elsewhere? And what are these factors in more recent times?

Darling's excellent analysis begins from a kind of Malthusian premise that land (and the local economy rooted in it) can only support a certain maximum population, which in the case of the West Highlands, was exceeded greatly as a result of the population upsurge in the Highlands during the second half of the eighteenth century. Other analysts would seem to agree that people began to leave the land in the Scottish Highlands as early as the middle or late eighteenth century even in advance of the Highland clearances.

This self-initiated response to the Malthusian problem of too many people on too little land and wherewithal was encouraged by the landlords, who subsequently aided and abetted the natural process of emigration, and who, in some well-known cases, forcibly evicted crofters and tenants who would not otherwise have chosen to leave the land. The combination of voluntary and forced migration was certainly in the best interests of the landlords of this time, for in the eighteenth and early nineteenth centuries, they faced problems because of changes in their own circumstances. To an increasing extent, the large Scottish landowners, the lairds, were becoming anglicized. They were being educated in England, they maintained residences in England, they sought favour in London-based social and political circles, and they needed money to support themselves in this way of life. Before the 1745 rising insured the demise of the clan system in the Highlands, the conditions which would bring this era of history to a close were already in place, and the curtain had begun to fall. The lairds no longer needed fighting men from their estates; they needed rents instead. Collections of rent, previously lax, became increasingly tight, and the amounts of the rents began to climb. At the same time, the common folk who lived on the land and worked it found themselves unable to meet the new demands. The land would yield no more, and there were more mouths to feed. Not only could they not cough up the rents as the new system demanded cash rather than clan loyalty, but the increasingly numerous common folk actually cost the laird more than depopulated land. When famine or disease struck, for example, the laird was expected to show enough of the old *noblesse oblige* to provide food and medicine to prevent an otherwise embarrassing death rate (although in some cases these necessities of life were made available as loans or sales on credit rather than as gifts, presumably so as not to encourage the further proliferation of the population). In short, it cost the laird to maintain his people on his estates, and at the same time he was gaining nothing in the way of money in return.

When sheep farming was introduced to the Highlands, it spread quickly because it was a solution to the laird's problems. The coming of the sheep in the late eighteenth century finished the historical process which had begun much earlier and set in train a new sequence of events. The landowners began to consolidate the farms they owned; fewer farms meant that fewer tenants were required. The management of these farms (by 'tacksmen'), which in earlier times would have been turned over to loyal kinsmen and supporters, was increasingly taken over by more 'professional' farm managers who were the successful bidders for the farms on an open market. The raising of stock—both sheep and cattle—began to be informed by the growing 'science' of agriculture, and new techniques and technologies began to replace the old 'dog and stick' methods of farming. The spread of sheep farming was the beginning of the rationalization and commercialization of agriculture in the Highlands, and this process of rationalization and 'improvement' seems to have taken place earlier in Argyll under the leadership of the Dukes of Argyll than in other parts of the Highlands.

The coming of the sheep accomplished two things for the landowners: it allowed landlords to expedite the process of depopulation, which had already begun, in the name of efficiency and progress, thereby cutting the cost to the lairds of maintaining an excessive non-productive population; and it gave the landlords some prospects of income from the sheep who displaced the people, and from the higher rents paid by more commerce-minded large-scale tacksmen and tenants.

The process of depopulation, once it began, continued through the whole of the nineteenth century (spurred again by the potato failures of 1846 and 1847) and through most of the twentieth, as we have seen. The cause of the continued emigration of people from the area is the same as it has been for about two hundred years. Once a cash economy was introduced into the countryside, it became more and more difficult to survive on subsistence farming. Unless a person could find a place as a commercial farmer, or could hire on for a wage as a farm labourer, or could find some other means of cash income through wages or sales of goods or services, he had to begin thinking of looking elsewhere to make a living. The opportunities for realizing income were not sufficient to support the population, despite the fact that the latter was decreasing. And so the people have continued to leave—for Glasgow, for Canada, for Australia, for America, and for England.

The government has for some decades now considered de-population of the countryside a social problem, especially in the Highlands. In the face of what seems to be an inexorable set of historical forces, and against difficult odds determined by the global economic and power relationships which make such regions as the Highlands marginal, various government agencies have organized policies and programmes which might help dam the flow of people. Various official commissions have over the years promulgated such policies for the Highlands. The report of the Scottish Economic Committee on the Highlands and Islands in 1938 is a good example of this long-standing concern about declining population. Early in the report, the Committee asserts in the high-sounding prose of officialdom that development of the Highlands is in the national interest:

> We submit that in view of the present trend towards concentration of population in the larger cities and industrial centres, the full development of an area such as the Highlands for the building up of a strong, healthy, and virile race must be regarded as being of vital importance to the nation . . .[6]

The key to the 'Highland problem' as it was understood by this body of notables was providing employment 'to re-establish a young and fully employed population'. Although the Committee confined development methods to those which were 'of assured practical value', it was recognized that some of the constraints of rigid economic rationality might have to be set aside in order to keep people on the land ('. . . it may be necessary to expend money in defiance of the laws of strict economics in order that an adequate and normal population shall be established and maintained . . .').

The Forestry Commission has for over sixty years played the role of national employer in peripheral areas of Great Britain. According to its own publication,[7] after 1958 'providing employment in rural areas where jobs are scarce' became an important social objective. In a list of twelve objectives published in 1980, there appears this one:

> To stimulate and support the local economy in areas of depopulation by the development of forests, including the establishment of new plantations, and of wood-using industry.[8]

The Commission even adds that in order to maintain employment, it will in some cases slow the pace of mechanization 'provided the increase in real cost can be kept down'.

Similarly, the Crofters Commission [established in 1955 to administer the Crofters (Scotland) Act of 1955][9] in carrying out its duties in developing and regulating crofting in Scotland, believes that crofting is important as one means of keeping people on the land. The Commission recognizes the part-time nature of crofting, and works with other agencies in the development of ancillary jobs for crofters, but it believes, nonetheless, that:

> Crofting is an essential ingredient in the regional economy of the Highlands and Islands as well as being a population anchor in peripheral areas.[10]

The Highlands and Islands Development Board has been explicit from its beginnings in 1965 about the goal of stemming depopulation, which it regarded as one of the major symptoms of 'the Highland problem.' In a recent publication, the HIDB refers to the early development of policy guidelines which included the following statement:

> Its overall objectives would be to attempt to halt depopulation in the region as a whole and in doing so 'to offer an alternative way of life to that in the great cities . . .'[11]

Lumb reminds her readers that Robert Grieve (now Sir Robert Grieve), the first HIDB chairman, believed that '. . . the Board will be judged by its ability to hold population in the true crofting areas'. She goes on to say that

> . . . this emphasis on the need to stem depopulation and maintain settlement in the remoter parts of the Highlands and Islands has been implicitly accepted as a major goal of the HIDB and much of its policy in the economic, industrial and social development fields has been formulated with a view to 'holding' people in the area.[12]

In the guidelines furnished by HIDB to those seeking financial assistance, the section on 'Criteria for Board Assistance' stresses, among other things, the importance of the criterion of additional employment which will be created and the remoteness of the location of proposed projects; this is the translation into practical terms of the Board's objective of stopping or reversing the outflow of people from the Highlands.[13]

It is important to review these examples of government policy and programmes to establish the widespread and longstanding acceptance of Highland depopulation as a fact and a social problem. Villages such as Ford have contributed to the outflow, like small streams which flow to rivers and ultimately to the sea.

But the residents of Ford do not view what has happened so much as part of a national problem as something which happens to them, their relatives and friends and neighbours, and to their village. Depopulation is more than an 'historic phenomenon' to people who still live with the memories of lost brothers and next-door neighbours, who can see empty houses and holiday homes where large farm families once filled them with activity, who are still saying farewells to family members leaving right now, this year, this week, to find a life elsewhere, and who hear their own feelings expressed in the words of the Ann Lorne Gillies song 'Always Argyll', popular in the winter of 1981.

Tosh Beaton is a young resident of Ford who can recall when he came as a child with his family to nearby Arichamish Farm in 1957. There were six Beatons, five McKinnons, and four Crearars living in the three houses on Arichamish in those days. Of that total of fifteen people, no one lives at Arichamish now. There are three Beatons left in Ford; there are none of the McKinnons of that family, or Crearars, left here. One of the three houses of Arichamish Farm is available for vacation renters; the other two are for sale again just now. The place broke up as a farm in 1970, with the land sold to the Forestry Commission and the houses placed on the open market by the Department of Agriculture, which owned it. This is a contemporary repetition of the same basic processes which drained Torranbeg a century before.

Tosh doesn't think of what happened to Arichamish as a 'phenomenon'—it isn't depopulation to him. It's just a plain fact about which he is not terribly sentimental. (When I asked him if he had considered leaving Ford, his answer was a satisfied, 'As long as there's Ford, that's where I'll be.') People have been leaving the area all of Tosh's life. It started long before he came on the scene and it may continue yet awhile. Whether he knows it now or wants to think about it, the probabilities of the demographer may catch up with Tosh himself sooner or later.

The outward flow has borne many—in fact most—of the children of the residents of Ford. The flow has taken mostly the young (and some would say the enterprising, but that is a conjecture difficult to prove). Nell Kerr, who came to Ford in 1948 with her late husband James, has seen her two children grow up and leave for work in Central Scotland. Lana and Gibby McCuig (Gibby was born at Ederline) have seen one daughter leave for work in England, and are about to see another one go at any time. Sheena Carmichael has watched her son John leave for college-level training in forestry, knowing that, as he himself put it, 'In a way, I've already left'. Betty McLean has one daughter aged 22 who has left the area, and another, 19, who may leave at any time.[14]

It is interesting to listen to people as they talk about people close to them leaving. There is great uniformity of understanding about why it happens. Sheena Carmichael knows that John—young, bright, vigorous, and well-trained—would be qualified for a post in the forest in which he grew up (Inverliever), but she *understands* what John means when he says, 'Of course I would prefer to stay here, but I must go where the work is.' 'The work' may take him to Perth or to Papua, New Guinea, but probably not to Ford. But Sheena is resigned to his leaving, knowing that it is for the best if he is to make his own way in the world; she has already learned to live alone, she says (she was widowed in 1974).

I asked Lana McCuig how Veronica felt about leaving Ford. (Veronica, 20, is a nanny in England.) 'She never gave it a thought.' How does Lana feel about her children leaving?

> I've encouraged them to get away as soon as they could. I've thumped it into them, in a way. There's nothing here for them. It's a good place for children to grow up, until they get about 14 or 15, and then they begin to think they're missing out on a lot of things they would get involved in if they lived in a town or city. John (15) is just beginning to get these feelings.

Liz, who is 16, will be the next to leave as soon as she finds employment as a nanny 'down south', hoping eventually to take nurses' training through the Army. Meanwhile, Liz has been helping in the hotel in the summer, waiting tables and cleaning rooms. Her boyfriend, the 17-year-old Willis boy from the nursery up the road, is preparing to leave, too, to go to Inverness-shire where he can get further training and experience in nursery work. He and his brother are both leaving Ford despite their father's ill health; the family all know it is ultimately for the best. Young Willis and Liz know that his leaving for the north and her leaving for the south will be a serious separation, too, but that it is necessary for their futures. They plan to meet again and marry in a few years, and everyone wishes them luck.

Betty McLean and her daughter Shirley confirm Lana's view that Ford is enjoyed by children only to a certain age. It is not a good place for young people after they reach high school age, they say, because there is no social life for them—no dances, no pictures, nothing for them to do. That is why most of them begin to get ideas about leaving.

The MacNays share a similar opinion.

> The young are leaving. What is there to keep them here? There are a few jobs, but they want better jobs than we can give them here. And young people today want more than just employment. They've seen television; they want the bright lights of the city. What they didn't see they didn't want. But they've seen it now. There's nothing here for the bright youth who are leaving. Or the duller young people, either.

These views about the lure of urban attractions and the inability of the country life to cater to the wants and needs of youth may work as statistical generalities, but they do not apply to every instance in Ford. Ruaridh Murray, who is 15, has not voiced any dissatisfaction with life in Ford, and in fact seems totally absorbed with the shooting, wildlife, boating, hotel work, and the association with country folk that living in Ford allows. John Carmichael, who is 22, has said that he would not be foregoing anything—except employment—by remaining in Ford; that is, he could live without the rapid advancement and without the urban amenities and be quite happy in Ford in the place he likes, with his people. Nor does Tosh Beaton feel that he has lost anything by remaining in Ford. So the 'bright lights' explanation, while it applied in many instances, does not apply to all.

I asked Hamish McNeill how he was handling the situation of his son James, who is 16 and stalking a future somewhere outside Ford. Hamish was matter-of-fact:

> James has shown some interest in the Merchant Navy. Fact, he's been interviewed already. He would get further training in engineering that way. (He wouldn't fancy anything manual.) There's no real possibility of him staying here. He'll have to go to get work. And he's keen to travel.

> I don't try to influence the children about work. Or about where to
> live. I think we should let them make up their own minds.

So while some 'thump' leaving into their children, others let them
work it out on their own. In none of my conversations did I hear of
any action taken by a parent in discouraging a child from leaving
the village. There is some sadness at leave-taking, of course, and
everyone predicts that all these children will be back eventually to
take up their retirement days in Ford, but most feel as Mrs Kerr
does, that the young must leave in order to find work elsewhere:

> We knew there was nothing for our children here, since Robin didn't
> want to follow farming. You know, leaving to go into the world is not
> so much a problem for children who grow up on a farm. They learn
> about life. Leaving was not a difficulty for our children. In fact,
> parents don't encourage their young enough to go out and stand on
> their own feet . . . I know that James (Mrs Kerr's late husband) tried
> to impress this upon Robin.

In short, the way the people of Ford look at it, most people have
to leave the village after their schooling in order to satisfy their
desires for careers, travel, and whatever advantages they might see
in urban life. The leaving, and the reasons for the leaving, are
understood, accepted, even applauded. The village is not awash in
sentimental tears. Leaving has been a fact of life too long; the
export for which the Highlands (indeed Scotland) is best known is
its people. The way depopulation is experienced in Ford is
something like death: it's sad, but there you are. It's part of life, and
when it happens, you just go on.

But the story of Ford is more than just one of *de*population. First
of all, the rate of migration may well have slowed since 1971, so
that it is possible Ford is retaining more of its people, especially the
young, than it has in recent decades. Second, and most important,
Ford and communities like it appear to be *re*populating. This part
of the story also deserves our attention, for this is a new
phenomenon in the history of the Highlands and, no matter whether
it is a short-term or a long-term trend, it will have lasting effects on
the makeup of the village and its way of life.

Hollingsworth has said that while the rate of out-migration is not
constant, it is less variable than the rate of in-migration.[15] The
growth of a community, in his view, is not so dependent on the rate

at which people leave as the rate at which they are coming in. In special cases where the rate of out-migration has been high for such a long time as that of the Highlands, his thesis makes sense; at least it forces our attention to a part of the equation we would otherwise ignore.

In-migration has long been a fact in Scotland as a whole in the Highlands as well as the rest of the country.[16] Bell and Kirwan show that between 1966 and 1971, the number of migrants from Scotland to the rest of the United Kingdom totalled around 167,000, while the number of migrants from the rest of the United Kingdom to Scotland was a surprising 124,000—a net loss of only 43,000 people.[17] Looking only at Argyll, in 1931 almost six percent of the county's population had been born outside Scotland, a proportion which grew to almost eight percent by 1951. Moreover, fully a third of the population of Argyll in these earlier years had been born elsewhere in Scotland, mostly in the Glasgow/Clydeside area.[18] Figures provided by the HIDB for Argyll and Bute for the years 1971-76 show that the population increased in the whole area from 63,057 to 65,615, an increase of 2,558. However, given that there was a natural decrease of population (because of the imbalance in the number of deaths over the number of births), the net migration into Argyll and Bute between those years was 3,314, or about one percent per year.[19] This remarkable statistic means that far more people were coming into the area than were leaving in the decade of the seventies. (Specifically, in the mid-Argyll area, with a population of 4,725, there were 325 in-migrants and 200 out-migrants in 1971.)[20]

Most of these people are moving into larger towns such as Lochgilphead and Oban, of course, both of which are growing rapidly at this time. Little Lochgilphead's astonishing overnight growth can be explained by the coming of the District Council headquarters to that town in the mid-nineteen-seventies, bringing 200 new families, and the concentration of certain Regional Authority offices there, which brought another 100 families. In addition, new industries have grown in the town, creating such a feeling of economic boom that there is no housing left for all the families wishing to live there. The housing overflow is being felt by nearby Ardrishaig, which has also reached its maximum capacity, and by Kilmichael, which is turning into a bedroom community for Lochgilphead.

But some of this in-migration is being experienced by the village of Ford as well. In fact, Ford is catching a small amount of the overflow from Lochgilphead and Ardrishaig, where no further housing can be built until new plans for water facilities can be approved. Out of the total number of households in Ford (59), 8 include a member of the family who works in Lochgilphead or Ardrishaig. Thus, although it is 12 miles distant, Ford has acquired a segment of commuters to Lochgilphead as part of its population. (In actuality, a 20-minute commute sounds very attractive to most people accustomed to longer driving times in the cities.)

Ford is not only absorbing some of the overflow from the town nearby, it is also increasing because there are people who find work in Ford, or who simply want to live in a place such as Ford and can afford to do so (or can afford to try). In other words, some were brought to the area because of their work and then found a place in Ford to live, while others specifically wanted to live in Ford (or a place like it) and then either waited for the opportunity to retire here or came on faith and sought gainful employment.

Some of the former are part of the boom in Lochgilphead which has caused its population to climb from 4,000 to 4,600 between 1971 and 1981 (Preliminary Census figures, 1981). In addition, there is at least one couple who have returned to Ford in their retirement, having left for work elsewhere in Scotland at an early age.

These variations in the circumstances of in-migration are borne out in conversations with Ford's newcomers. Joachim Brolly moved to Ford in 1975 after he emigrated from Ireland in 1972. He married a Tarbert girl, went to work for the Forestry Commission, and found that the only house the Commission had available for them to rent was in Ford. He bought his own winch and went into the private timber contracting business in 1976. Within a year, he says, 'I knew I was on the right track.' His brother Jude joined him, and he bought two more winches. He now has two large timber trucks and five winches and works 31 men. He sees no end to the work in timber around Ford, and he plans to stay there indefinitely. He is looking for a house to buy.

James Brotherston is from Glasgow originally, although he worked most of his life in Newcastle. He liked the Ford area and chose to retire here five years ago when he was 60. He is employed on a part-time basis as the caretaker for the Inverliever Trust Lodge.

The Milnes came to Ford in 1972 to work for Ederline Estate. Originally from Perthshire, Charles Milne has worked in the Highlands for many years, and came to this village for the work it afforded.

The Poupards, from England, moved to Creaganterve in 1975 when he became part of the management of the Shell Oil Company-controlled fish farm at Ardrishaig.

Nostalgia and family feeling brought the Greenshields to Scotland from England. Mr Greenshields' grandfather was from near Edinburgh, and he could recall his grandmother talking about Scotland, although she had only been there once. The family came to the Highlands on many pleasure trips and then began looking around Dundee and then Appin for a place to which to retire eventually. They learned about a lot for sale at Ford from the Forestry Commission, from whom they bought it. They knew of Ford from earlier tours taken in the nineteen-fifties. Mr and Mrs Greenshields and his sister, Miss Greenshields, retired from teaching in Wales and built their present home in Ford in 1975. They have opened a guest house in part of their home, and by filling the four guest rooms frequently enough, they have been able to pay off their bank loan sooner than they expected.

Andy Moffat and his wife, Val, came to Ford in 1978. He wanted a place in the Oban area and was not particular where; he just needed to be in the north because his work as a geologist required him to be near the North Sea oil fields. He wanted to live on the west side of the country rather than the east because he could be called to work too easily if he lived in the east. As it is, his work now takes him to the south and out of the country rather than to the North Sea, but as of now he has no plans to move from Ford. Andy's father was from Arrochar, on Loch Long, not far from here, but this fact, he says, had no influence on choosing a place to live. While Andy commutes to his work via the four-times weekly helicopter service from Lochgilphead to Glasgow, Val commutes to her teaching job in Lochgilphead itself. They are both originally from London.

Basil and Dolly MacNay retired to Ford from England in 1968, but they first began to visit the West Highlands in 1959. They came to Ford frequently on holidays over a long period and became good friends with the Murrays. They had come to know everyone in the village by that time, and had also been 'sized up' by the people of Ford, too. It was just the place they had in mind for retirement.

Tommy and Renee Alston also retired to Ford, moving into the house next to the Greenshields in 1980. Tommy is originally from Glasgow, Renee from Yorkshire, England. Tommy had travelled in the West Highlands for many years as part of his work. They knew they wanted to retire somewhere in the area. They saw the advertisement for their present home in the *Oban Times*. They had looked at other sites in villages such as Tayvallich but found the lots too small.

James McNair and his wife Nan moved into their new house on 'The Row' in 1973. Mr McNair was born in Ford, at Creaganterve Farm, but his family left here when he was only 11 months old. Why did he come here to live again? 'I really belong here. My family have been here for generations. It's funny the way people come back.' He has been a successful farmer at Achnamara (less than twenty-five miles from Ford) in the intervening years. He has worked very hard all his life and now has the financial means to retire near the McNair homeland.

Ralph and Lucy Clough, like some of the other newcomers to Ford, came here somewhat by chance. They are from England, but were living in Wales at the time they first came to the Highlands for a vacation visit to Mrs Clough's sister. They had no idea of looking for a place while they were here, but they happened to park next to the real estate agent's office in Lochgilphead and went in on impulse. The agent warned them that of the two properties currently available, the one in Ford might be disappointing—most viewers, he said, came back from Ford complaining of the rain, the small size, and so on. They were at that stage of life when they wanted a home of their own, having lived in rented or 'tied' houses up to that time. They made an offer on the 'Change-house' and moved into it the next summer without jobs. That was in 1975.

Lucy works in adult education in Lochgilphead now; Ralph worked in the town for one year, and since then he has put together a creative patchwork of free-lance teaching jobs which keep him busy in Ford and the surrounding area. Looking back on that day in 1974, Ralph says with the voice of experience, 'Life's most important decisions seem to be made on impulse.'

Roger Park came with his wife, Nan, to Ford in 1973. He is originally from Ayrshire, but he has travelled extensively with the Merchant Navy, and has spent several years living in other parts of the West Highlands. Before coming to Ford, the Parks lived for a year on an island off nearby Ardfern. Roger is interested in local lore and history, and characterizes himself as 'a scenery nut', describing the district around Ford as 'God's country'. Roger came to work in a fish farm in 1973, and when the firm closed and he was given his severance pay, he used it to go into business as a mechanic in a garage next to the hotel.

Virtually all the farmers in Ford are recent incomers. In addition to the Milnes, there are the McKinnons at Torran and the McKenzies at Creaganterve. The McKinnons came to Ford from the Kintyre peninsula to the south, giving up their farm there and being offered Torran by the Forestry Commission. His lease is for ten years, but farmers who show they can work their farms productively and can pay the rent are seldom put out, says McKinnon. The McKenzies, Geordie and Sheena, are in their twenties. They have been in Ford only two years as shepherds for Nigel Boase, who owns Creaganterve and rents the land at Auchinellan. They moved to Ford from the island of Mull for their work.

Indeed, the only long-time residents of Ford who are and have been farming are Alasdair McNair, who works his father's farm at Stroneskir, and Iain Cumming, who helps McKinnon farm Torran. Both are Ford natives.

Iain Cumming and Alasdair McNair and his father, Alex, who is now in his eighties, are in fact among the few persons in Ford who can claim the status of native. Almost everyone who lives here now was born somewhere else. David Murray once made the claim that

> Everyone who now lives in Ford is an incomer, although some have lived here for thirty years. You'll not find a native any older than I.

David is 45 years old. I have found only five persons in Ford who would disprove his claim: Maimie Cameron, the Postmistress, who was born at Salachry Farm around sixty years ago; Ruby Campbell, who was born in 1908 and grew up on Braevallich Farm and Ederline Estate; Alex McNair of Stroneskir Farm; and Iain Cumming, in his sixties, a shepherd at Torran Farm. (And James McNair, who lived outside Ford from the time he was one year old until his retirement.) Others in Ford who can claim nativity (aside from the children) could be counted on one hand, and they are all younger than 45.

This is the most surprising fact of life in Ford: *it has been almost entirely repopulated by incomers over the years.* Whether the phenomenon of repopulation is found in other areas of the Highlands I do not know, but I would guess that this evidence of high mobility is not confined to one village in Argyll. Most of the historical and demographic literature concerning population movement in the Highlands concentrates on depopulation through emigration and low rates of natural increase. In at least this one small place in the West Highlands, that is no longer even half the story; the village of Ford is alive today only because of the movement of people into it. For some time now, it has come nowhere close to reproducing itself, and yet over the past few years its population has increased. One other social scientist who has noticed and written about this trend, Rosemary Lumb, states that 'incomers are certainly the most significant element in the changing migration patterns of the Highlands and Islands.'[21]

What evidence is there of population increase in Ford itself? Fortunately, when the ladies of the SWRI wrote their local history in 1965 and 1966, they furnished a count of the population by age group, as shown in Table 5-2.[22]

Table 5-2
Population of Ford, by age, 1966

Age	Number
Children under school age	7
Children under 11	9
11-16	6
17-20	7
21-30	24
31-65	39
Over 65 years	17
Total:	109

Fifteen years later, in November 1981, the count appeared as given in Table 5-3.

Table 5-3
Population of Ford, by Age and Sex, 1981

Age	# Male	# Female	Total
0-4	7	5	12
5-11	6	2	8
12-16	12	9	21
17-20	7	3	10
21-30	11	8	19
31-40	7	8	15
41-50	13	12	25
51-60	6	7	13
61-70	8	12	20
Over 70	5	8	13
Total:	82	74	156

The increase in the population of Ford over the past decade and a half is clear from these figures: it has gone up by almost fifty percent. The more recent numbers also permit some analysis of changes in the age composition of the population of Ford. It is a commonly accepted assumption among Ford residents that the village is 'top-heavy', that it is an 'elderly community' because of the combined effects of young people departing and older couples without children migrating here for their retirement years. One man put this view starkly when he expressed his opinion that the important distinction in Ford was that between 'breeders' and 'non-breeders', and that the breeders had been replaced by a succession of non-breeders. While it is certainly true that a number of retirement age and childless people have moved into Ford in recent years, the figures show that the age structure is somewhat more balanced in 1981 than it was in 1966. While the categories are not precisely comparable, almost 16 percent of the population in 1966 was over 65 years of age, compared to 8 percent over 70 in 1981. In 1966, 20 percent of the population was under 17; the figure for 1981 was 26 percent. Twenty-seven percent of the people were under 20 years of age in 1966, compared to 33 percent 20 and under in 1981. The proportion of pre-schoolers is also up slightly in 1981. The *Statistical Account* of 1794 indicated that almost half the population of the parish was under 20 years of age. While the population of Ford today does not duplicate the proportions of the late eighteenth century, it is not quite as 'top-heavy' as it was a few years ago.

The reason for this fact is that working-age people have been moving into Ford alongside those of retirement age. Ralph and Lucy Clough, for example, brought their three children with them, and Duncan McKinnon and his wife brought two of their children. Jeff and Jesse Smith have two children, as do the McKenzies. Two of Betty McLean's children live with her in Ford. And so on. The widespread view that Ford holds of itself as a 'retirement village' is exaggerated. It is true that young people are leaving and that retired couples are moving in, but the effects of these patterns are substantially offset by the presence of other, working-age couples—both recent incomers and those of longer standing in the village—with children. From at least a demographic standpoint, Ford does not appear to be dying, but growing just a bit younger.

As was indicated earlier, of the 70 dwellings standing in Ford in 1981, 59 were occupied. Table 5-4 shows the breakdown of these households by the age of the dwelling, the native/incomer status, and recency of arrival of the occupants.

The figures in this table lead to some rather striking observations. The most remarkable fact is that 33 of the 59 households are those of recent incomers. *Over half of the households in Ford have been set up by incomers within the past 12 years.* Also, in confirmation of the only slightly exaggerated claim of David Murray, there are only 7 native heads of households among the 59, which means that *88 percent of Ford's households are occupied by incomers of one generation or another.*

Table 5-4

Age of Occupied Dwellings, Native/Incomer Status, and Recency of Arrival of Occupants

Year Dwelling was Built	Native	Incomer		Total
		Pre-1970	1970-81	
Pre-1950	3	11	7	21
1950-59	—	2	6	8
1960-69	3	4	2	9
1970-81	1	2	18	21
Total:	7	19	33	59

Almost equally remarkable is the young age of much of Ford's occupied housing and the extent to which it is associated with incoming. Eighteen of the 21 dwellings built or totally renovated since 1970 are occupied by households which have arrived in Ford since 1970. One-third of the occupied housing in Ford is 12 years old or less, and it is almost entirely occupied by recent incomers. (Of the 11 unoccupied dwellings, three are holiday homes, two are second homes; four of them have been built since the late 1960s.)

Aside from increasing the population, expanding the housing, and influencing the age structure, what other effects has the presence of incomers had on Ford? Two sets of consequences are worth examining: the effects of incomers on social organizations in the village, and the effects of incomers on divisions within the community.

Insofar as the collective life of Ford is expressed in its formal organizations—and to a great but not exclusive extent it is—then the conclusion is inescapable that the recent incomers to Ford have played a prominent role in collective life. It was the initiative of a newcomer with small children which was behind the start of the play group in 1981. Recent incomers also play important roles in the church; one is an elder and another plays the organ. Incomers have been active, along with longer-term residents, on the Village Hall Committee since before the Hall was built, and indeed they helped to get it built. It was recent incomers who initiated the Badminton Club and the Youth Club. Recent incomers participate vigorously in the fund-raising whist drives and sales of work. They join with the longer-term residents in the Ford Gun Club shoots. In the past they have been part of the Keep Fit Club and the weekly country dancing which faded from the scene in recent years. It was recent incomers who attempted to start a club for older persons and a baby clinic. Recent incomers also helped secure the cable television antenna for the village, although the leadership seems to have come from longer-term residents.

In short, the incomers have had an undeniably invigorating effect on village organizations. They are carrying a considerable share of the collective load. Not only in formal organizations but in informal help as well, the recent incomers are conspicuous in their work on behalf of others in Ford.

A longer-term resident summed up the feelings of an appreciative segment of the community by saying:

> We've always loved Ford. Everything around Ford and the estates is lovely. But we always found a kind of deadness about Ford. Many people haven't really lived, if you know what I mean, and they don't want to make changes. Without the incomers, the village would have gone to sleep again. Having incomers is an excellent thing. They blend in well. They give of themselves. It's a shame that some don't take advantage of them coming here.

Others in the village echo this sentiment, remarking that Ford simply would not be the same without these incomers.

This brings us to the second consequence of the presence of recent incomers in Ford: the new division in the community which it has precipitated. There are many in the community who would agree completely that the place would not have been the same without the incomers—but some claim it would have been better without them.

Feelings about recent incomers run the entire spectrum of human feeling, from the expression of praise and gratitude at one end to statements of rank disaffection at the other. It is not a thing that is made public in the sense of face-to-face argument and conflict, but the feelings of almost everyone are known to everyone else through the magic of small-town communication. What some find a positive asset to the village, others find offensive. What some regard as community leadership which brings new life to the village, others see as outsiders imposing their own ways on Ford.

The English incomers are a special target of negative feelings; the larger context of anti-English sentiment must be understood to put this matter in perspective, and we will return to it shortly. In my second visit to Ford, I learned about these feelings very quickly. I asked one person what the present population of Ford was, and was told that it had recently increased 'because of incomers from the south (England) who are buying up houses and property as local people die off or move out, at prices the local people can't afford.' I was told by someone else on the same visit that 'they' come in 'with their own ways of doing things and want to change it here. They are not used to our country ways.' Another person remarked, in the same vein, 'You know how we must feel when people come through here and ask how we can stand all this peace and quiet.'

On another occasion, I asked how the renovation of the old farmhouse at Torran Mor came about. It was explained that when Logie Richmond, the farmer, died, an appeal was made to the County Council to convert it into flats. 'Local people' now live there. If this had not been done, someone from outside would have bought it and fixed it over to sell or let to 'you know who'.

A recent emigrant from Ford once observed that he thought some of the incomers must have had experience in the colonies and came here with colonialist attitudes about the locality and its residents, treating them as though they were backward and knew nothing. Thus, he said, they took the lead in community organizations and did so in a manner which did not endear them to the locals. In this manner they earned themselves the label 'white settlers'.

The term 'white settlers' can be heard frequently in Ford as well as in other parts of the Highlands and perhaps elsewhere in Scotland,[23] but it is not a term used by or appreciated by all or even most long-term residents. As one woman put it, 'The term "white settlers" is used here, but it's really not fair. The incomers have been good for the village in a way.' It is indeed a term of harsh derision—not one that would be used in the company of an English incomer—and it reveals the depth of feelings of some about what they think is happening to their place.

A Scottish incomer summed up the feelings of many when he said:

> Scottish folk are easy-osy. The English want to come in and do things different—their way.

Even when the English try to do things the Scottish way—and many demonstrate a serious interest in local history and lore—they are still English. More than one Scottish resident seemed to take pleasure in the struggle some of the English were having with the Gaelic. A native, for example, commented that 'The English name their houses in Gaelic, but they can't spell it or pronounce it.' (It needs to be said, however, that many of the Scots have their own problems with Gaelic.)

The attitude of many Scots towards the English has a long history. The Act of Union in 1707 brought the two countries together voluntarily as one nation, which placed relations between Scotland and England on a more peaceable basis than those between England and Ireland, which was first conquered and then brought into the national fold. But the union with England was more voluntary for some than others in Scotland, especially in the Highlands. The Risings of 1715 and 1745 showed that there were strong elements of resistance throughout the country, and the brutality with which the '45 Rising was put down by the Duke of Cumberland reveals the degree of anxiety the English felt about the threat from the north. There are Scots today who are mindful of the aftermath of the '45—the imprisonment, the butchery, the banning of the kilt. Moreover, the English come in for their share of the blame for certain uncharitable acts committed in the name of 'improvement'. Today the English are blamed for everything from inflation and unemployment to emigration and the U.S. nuclear arms parked in Scotland.

It is difficult to say how deep or widespread this anti-English sentiment is. There are many Scots who are proud of their Scottishness and their Britishness at the same time, while there are others working actively for the cause of complete independence from England. The Scottish National Party has fed on this sentiment for many decades, at some times feeding more successfully than at others. Letters to the editor in *The Scotsman* and the *Glasgow Herald* allow daily ventings of pro-Scottish and anti-English feelings, whether the topic be the real meaning of Guy Fawkes Day, the loss of a Gaelic teacher on Skye, low-flying practice by Jaguars and F-111s through the glens of the Highlands, or the confounding of the adjectives 'British' and 'English'.[24] The social scientists who have written on the subject of Scottish nationalism have seemed sometimes to miss the complexity of such sentiments and have failed to appreciate the range of possible directions and depths of anti-English feeling. It is first here and then it is there, as it were, and in some years the noise is quite loud (e.g., early 1979) and then it seems to be only a few voices crying alone.

The feeling has existed in varying intensities in Scotland for centuries, probably harboured more closely by the Gaelic remnant in the Highlands than by others, but it spills over into other areas, including the very heart of Campbell (which means anti-Jacobite) country, Argyll—and, even more specifically, Ford. It is an understandable, if not always very reasonable, sentiment. It sometimes seems, as my informant said about the term white settlers, 'really not very fair'.

Much of the anti-English feeling in Ford, however, is relatively light-hearted. Where there is humour, there is at least as much hope as there is meanness. One person enjoyed telling me about the time an Englishman stopped a long-time resident of Ford and asked, 'Where does this road go?' The Scotsman's answer, in case the reader is ever tempted to ask the same question, was, 'Nowhere. It stays right where it is.' On another occasion an Englishman asked a native woman, 'What do you do when it stops raining here?' He was told,'We just sit here and wait for it to rain again.'

Indeed, when I pressed one individual in Ford to assess the seriousness of the division between 'white settlers' and others, he said:

> Though it may sound so, there is no real hostility—or very little. I don't know whether they are aware of the feelings toward them. But it is not all that serious; their behaviour is regarded with amusement by most.

There are many in Ford who would agree that the hostility between the Scots and English is not great. The resentment is nonetheless sufficiently salient to create an ill-defined division within the community. It is ill-defined because the 'white settlers' are hardly ever singled out by name; one can guess who they are from strong inferences. It is ill-defined, as any stereotype will be because it generalizes too glibly and sweepingly, catching people in its net who do not belong there, perhaps missing some who do belong.

One would judge, from the talk among the longer-term residents, for instance, that Ford had experienced a veritable flood of English incomers in recent years, when in fact if there has been a flood at all, it has been a Scottish and not an English one. Table 5-5 gives the nativity and recency of incoming for all households in Ford in November 1981; the number of natives is also shown for comparison. It shows that of the 33 recent incomer households, 22 are Scottish and 9 English. Of the total of 52 incomer households, disregarding the date of arrival, 39, or 75 percent, are Scottish, and only 11, or 21 percent, are English.[25] Nine of the 11 households with an English head have moved into Ford in the last 12 years, and it may be the recency of this upsurge in the number of English residents which gives salience to the matter of nationality. But the number and proportion of English families eligible for the contemptuous label of 'white settler' is quite small.

Table 5-5

Nativity and Recency of Incoming of
Household Heads in Ford, 1981

Nativity	Pre-1970	1970-81	Total
English	2	9	11
Irish	—	2	2
Scottish	17	22	39
Total:	19	33	52
Native:			7
		Total:	59

Similarly, some longer-term residents in Ford expressed their belief to me that incomers 'from the south' are buying up houses and property, displacing local people. This does not seem to be the case among at least the older houses: of the 21 occupied pre-1950 dwellings, 18 are occupied by Scots, 14 of whom are either native or pre-1970 incomers, and only three are occupied by English families.

The tendency for the English incomers to group together residentially in 'The Row' also appears to be exaggerated by some Ford residents who expressed this opinion to me. There are 10 residents in 'The Row,' or 8 if the Forestry Commission's Nursery cottage duplex is set aside. Only three are occupied by households with English heads. The other English families are scattered literally from one end of Ford to the other. But the view seems to persist that 'The Row' is mostly English, as evidenced in the fact that one Scottish incomer overheard a chance remark in the village that a vacant house in 'The Row' had been bought by 'another English family' (the hearer was himself the purchaser).

But stereotypes and exaggerated views constitute evidence of an important social division which people carry in their heads and, to some extent, communicate to each other. The division does not express itself in most of the community's formal organizations, where the English and the Scots share in the leadership and in participation in a very balanced fashion. Nor does it cut in any clean, knife-like way through friendships, for it is certainly not the case that English are only friends with English and Scots with Scots. There may be a minority of Scots who are not close friends with any English (although they would still be friendly to them), and there is outright animosity in one relationship between a Scottish and an English family, but that is all. The division finds some expression in the tendency for the English not to participate in pub life, but there are exceptions to this generalization, and quite a number do drop by the bar for meals or come to pick up their Sunday newspapers at other than pub times.[26]

The visible evidence of the division between English and Scots is faint at best. 'The division' is too ill-constructed to be workable, spreading out as it does in some cases, to include recent incomers of every nationality, placing an artificial wedge between otherwise natural friendships and working relationships. The stereotype is too awkward to be useful at close quarters in everyday life in a small village. And so it remains latent. It is a new undercurrent, a changed condition of the atmosphere, a tiny crack in the ground where the people of Ford walk. The crack remains covered most of the time. It has to. As a recent Scottish incomer sagely observed:

> This is a one-street town—one shop, one bar, one post office—and you meet everyone almost every day. You have to be friendly because you know you're going to meet them again.

In this section we have looked closely at the depopulation of Ford and what it means to the village, and we have examined the evidence of repopulation, a dramatic new trend which is taking place in a number of Highland villages. Ford is growing, and the new mix of people has implications for the way life is lived in the village. It points to a new possible future for Ford, one which would not have been imagined just a few years ago. In the next section we try to explore what Ford means to its residents, new and old, and what people in and outside of the village think its future really is.

Footnotes

[1]Fraser Darling, (ed.), *West Highland Survey, An Essay in Human Ecology* (Oxford: Oxford University Press, 1955), p. 127. Also see the Scottish Economic Committee, *The Highlands and Islands of Scotland: A Review of the Economic Conditions with Recommendations for Improvement*, publ. 1938, p. 151.

[2]John Bryden and George Houston, *Agrarian Change in the Scottish Highlands*, Glasgow Social and Economic Studies No. 4 (London: Martin Robertson in connection with the HIDB, 1976), Chapter 3.

[3]Even if the Highland and Island population has become stabilized, it may be only a temporary phenomenon attributable to short-term trends such as escalating employment in the development phase of the oil industry. It should also be kept in mind that even with the recently experienced gains, Highlands and Islands population is a small fraction of the whole of Scotland—approximately five percent in 1975, compared to 48 percent who live in the Strathclyde (mainly composed of Glasgow) Region. See M. Gaskin, D.I. MacKay, Alison Marr, and N.F. Trimble, 'The Economic Impact of North Sea Oil on Scotland', Edinburgh, HMSO (1978), Chapter 6.

[4]*Census 1981, Scotland, Preliminary Report* (Edinburgh: HMSO, July 1981), p. 62. The figures quoted earlier for the 'Highlands and Islands' cannot be compared directly with those for the 'Highland Region,' because they are somewhat different geographic areas. The former includes everything that would be included in the Highlands Region, a regional governmental authority, but would also include Argyll, which is a district within the Strathclyde Region. To confuse matters further, the 'Highlands and Islands' area, which is the area of jurisdiction of the Highlands and Islands Development Board, is coterminous with the seven traditional crofting counties.

[5]*Ford and District*, (Oban: *Oban Times*, n.d. [circa 1966]), p. 49.

[6]Scottish Economic Committee, *The Highlands and Islands of Scotland: A Review of the Economic Conditions with Recommendations for Improvement* (Great Britain: Scottish Economic Committee Publications, 1938), p. 27.

[7]Forestry Commission, 'The Forestry Commission's Objectives', Edinburgh, June 1980 (Policy and Procedure Paper No. 1).

[8]*Ibid.*, p. 10.

[9]The Crofters Commission has its origin much earlier than 1955. Beginning with the Crofters Holdings (Scotland) Act of 1886, various governments have attempted through generations of agencies such as the Crofters Commission and the Highlands and Islands Development Board to respond to the problems of the region. For the historical background which led to the first Crofters act, see James Hunter, *The Making of the Crofting Community* (Edinburgh: John Donald, 1976).

[10]'Committee on Enquiry into the Acquisition and Occupancy of Agricultural Land', Memorandum by the Crofters Commission, n.d. (circa 1978), p. 21. Also see *The Crofters Commission Annual Report for 1980* (Edinburgh: HMSO, 1981).

[11]HIDB, 'The Highlands and Islands, A contemporary Account', Inverness, HIDB (February 1979), section 10-4.

[12]Rosemary Lumb, *Migration in the Highlands and Islands of Scotland*, University of Aberdeen Institute for the Study of Sparsely Populated Areas, Research Report No. 3 (October 1980), p. 1.

[13]HIDB, 'Financial Assistance', Inverness (1981), p. 4.

[14]By giving these examples of people who have recently left Ford, I do not want to imply that *every* child leaves Ford when he or she reaches a certain age, but it is true that *most* have done so. (The next largest number have left Ford but remain in Argyll or in the Highlands and Islands area. The smallest proportion consists of those who, like Tosh Beaton and Robert Gillies, have stayed in Ford.)

[15]T.H. Hollingsworth, *Migration, A Study Based on Scottish Experience between 1939 and 1964* (Edinburgh: Oliver and Boyd, 1970), p. 45.

[16]See the Scottish Economic Committee Report, *op. cit.,* the appendices of which provide data on emigration and immigration from about 1860 to 1930.

[17]D.N.F. Bell and F.X. Kirwan, 'Return Migration in a Scottish Context', *Regional Studies*, Vol. 3, No. 1 (1979), 101-111.

[18]*Third Statistical Account of Scotland, Argyll* (Glasgow: Collins, 1961), p. 81.

[19]HIDB, 'The Highlands and Islands . . .', *op. cit.*, Appendix, Table 2.

[20]*Census 1971, Scotland, Migration Tables (100%)*, p. 2.

[21]Rosemary Lumb, *op. cit.*, p. 140.

[22]*Ford and District*, *op. cit.*, p.49.

[23]Ralph Glasser, *Scenes from a Highland Life* (London: Hodder and Stoughton, 1981).

[24]Just as an example, and not at all an unusual one, this letter appeared in the December 4, 1981 *Scotsman* which happened to arrive while this writing was underway:

'I think the real cause of our present dilemma is that for far too long Scotland has presented a tragic picture of a "Kingdom divided against itself." The Declaration of Arbroath could be a source of inspiration, but it could also be a source of embarrassment. "For as long as a hundred of us are left alive we will never submit to England," yet we tamely acquiesce in the supremacy of the Westminster Parliament in which Scots representatives can be heavily outvoted by English representatives. Added to which some of our countrymen actually claim that we are far better off being governed from England than we would be if we governed ourselves.

'There are also a good many who think it is time a stand was made for Scotland, but when it comes to the test, they are too easily brought to heel, and they are powerless to break loose from the shackles of their anglicised upbringing.

'I wish the Scots would give the matter serious consideration for the sake of their beautiful country, their culture, their heritage, their folklore, their traditions and their way of life.

H.R. Baillie'

[25]The proportions are similar when individuals are counted rather than households. See Appendix Table 6.

[26]Compare with Howard Newby's description of the division between 'locals and newcomers' in the English village in his *Social Change in Rural England* (Madison: University of Wisconsin Press, 1979), pp. 164–172.

6 Ford Tomorrow:
Survival, Continuity, and Change

I believe in the beloved community
and in the spirit which makes it
beloved, and in the communion of all
who are, in will and deed, its members.
I see no such community as yet, but
nonetheless my rule of life is: Act
so as to hasten its coming.
Josiah Royce, quoted in
Roland L. Warren, 'The
Good Community—What
Would It Be?'

To ponder the future of the village of Ford is to consider the lives of all such communities everywhere. The issues upon which its life or death turn are at one level the same issues which confront and tranform small places in many nations.

'Life' and 'death' are, of course, metaphoric terms, taken from a biological context (where their meanings are obscure enough already) and applied, sometimes uncritically, by sociologists, anthropologists, journalists, and other observers of the human scene to forms of human association whose organic qualities have led thinkers to confuse communities with living organisms. Communities do not live as organisms live, and they do not die as organisms die, but it is nonetheless true that some localities seem to thrive while others wither—and sometimes disappear altogether. The metaphors of life and death have their uses as well as their limits.

To 'die' can mean something quite different in the case of a community in contrast with dying organisms. For example, dying, according to some writers, can become a permanent state of being, a form of association in its own right.[1] Thus, only to exist may not be sufficient to qualify a community for the term 'living'.

To what signs should we look, then, in determining whether places such as Ford are living or dying? Without intending to stretch the metaphor beyond its limits, we can ask what should be examined as signs of life in small communities, and by implication, we shall be asking what, in the absence of these signs, constitutes death. With answers to these questions, however tentative, the specific question of the future of Ford (and places like it) can be addressed more systematically and concretely.

At the very minimum, the living community requires, as a necessary pre-condition, humans inhabiting a locality. But people living in a bounded space do not necessarily constitute a communal form of association; that is, people living in proximity do not by virtue of this make a place a community. People in propinquity can be almost completely atomized, separated from each other by social space, living their lives, as in certain bedroom 'communities', almost totally in social orbits which pull them into patterns of work, friendship, and affiliation dominated by centres outside the locality of their households. Thus, the fact of people occupying a delimited space is only a minimal requirement for community.

In common parlance, those communities said to be thriving are those growing in size, while those that are 'dying' are the ones declining in population. (Those which witness little or no change in size are presumably in 'stable condition'. While it is unarguable that a shrinking population will ultimately disappear if the decline is unchecked, it is not necessarily true that increase equals life. Growth may breed business expansion, cause new buildings to be built, multiply roads, swell the schools, and increase the town budget. Growth may bring the social amenities and all those attributes we like to associate with modern town living. But by itself, growth may not increase community life: it may not (probably will not) increase the coherence of neighbourhoods, make it more likely to solve shared problems collectively, or reduce the perception of social separation from other members of the community. It is, therefore, misleading to associate population increase closely with community vitality. It may be enough simply to say that the absence of continued decline is a necessary pre-condition of good community health.

Aside from such pre-conditions, at what kinds of evidence should we look to find signs of health and vitality—the 'vital signs' of community? From experience and from an examination of the ideas of others who have concerned themselves with this question,[2] I suggest the following five community life signs should be considered:

1 The presence of shared, purposeful activity related to the collective interest of those inhabiting the locality.
2 The presence of locality-based institutions, or organized patterns of living.
3 The presence of shared identity rooted in a sense of place.
4 The presence of at least some minimal degree of authority over part of the decision-making which affects the locality.
5 The presence of shared overall goals and values regarding the community.

Each of these items deserves a brief word of explanation.

Vitality would seem to require a degree of shared, purposeful activity, the goals of which are related in some fashion to the locality. In plainer English, there is life in the community whose members get together to work on something which has to do with the community itself. There is less vitality in the community whose members are highly active solely on their own behalves, but where there is no shared work toward a 'common good'. Where there is evidence of apathy, fatalism, or cynicism about communal good and the work required to achieve it, there are signs of dying. The emphasis in this criterion of vitality is on the sharing of action, the working out of problems together, the working toward realized definitions of the good of the community among those who live there.

Another related expression of community vitality is the presence of locality-based institutions and organized living patterns. When people associate with each other in patterned and repetitive ways, are the sources and objects of the association relevant to the locality, or are they oriented to some other, non-local centre? The *origin* of a patterned association can, of course, be outside the community while the *object* can be internal, as would be the case with churches and schools. But the fundamental issue has to do with the bringing of people together in some patterned and regular relationship, the intended or unintended object of which relates to the locality.

A third sign of life in a community would seem to have to do with shared identity rooted in a sense of place. The sense of belonging is not, of course, exclusive: humans typically express *belonging* in a large number of social contexts simultaneously. We can belong to many groups concurrently and draw our identities from all of them. *Place* is one of these potential sources of attachment, belonging, and identity (indeed, it is possible to feel strong attachments to more than one place at a time, or to concentric places).

The sense of place is a complex and unexplored area of study, about which more will be said below. I do not think we understand much about how identification with place happens; indeed, it does not always happen. Somehow the felt uniqueness of a locality will become translated into a shared perception of specialness which is the source of group identity in that community. Where this occurs, there is another sign of life. Where it is weak or absent, there is less, or no vitality. Shared, purposeful activity will certainly have some effect on the level of shared sense of place and vice-versa, and both will be a cause and an expression of institutional patterns which are locality-relevant, so that none of the three life signs discussed so far is really independent of the others.

An issue discussed by some as the key to the life or death of small communities is that of the extent of local authority over decision-making.[3] It is difficult in this rudimentary stage of development of theories of life and death in communities to discern which are causes and which are symptoms of dying, but I am inclined to believe that a reduction in local control over the affairs of the community may be both. At the least, it constitutes an insidious, long-term trend which undermines other vital signs. While it may not operate as the sole cause of the decline of locality-based associations, it is unquestionably a powerful and pervasive one. Local control erodes to the extent that communications and transportation networks have grown more efficient, facilitating the control of peripheral areas from centralized (usually urban) localities. Whether cause or symptom or both, the relative absence of control by localities over the making of decisions which affect them as collective associations is anything but a sign of community vitality. But few communities have ever enjoyed complete autonomy. On a scale which reaches from the one extreme of total control to the other of absolutely no control over local affairs, there are none in the contemporary world which comes close to achieving the maximum. Any actual community today must be measured against what is probable rather than against what is theoretically possible.

Shared core values would seem to be another vital sign in a living community. I do not mean by this that there need be consensus on each and every matter which comes before the residents of a locality; uniformity of opinion in fact has a deadening aspect, and the extreme desire to achieve it leads to totalitarianism. Opposition and argumentation are healthy signs—if the argument is contained within agreed-upon boundaries and if it does not become an end in itself. It is the agreement upon over-reaching goals and values (domain assumptions) which is important to the life of a community. Where conflict is unbounded, we may be certain that community vitality has, at least for the duration, ebbed.

I am purposefully vague about the *degree* to which a community would have to register positively on each of these criteria in order to qualify as a 'good community'. I agree with Roland Warren that we have not thought sufficiently about the consequences of some of our idealized sentiments regarding community life. The pursuit of certain of these goals to an extreme would doubtless be intolerable, and some goals are in fact inconsistent with others. Let us simply say that the presence of these signs of life in *some* degree is required for vitality.

With this discussion as background, we can return to the question of the possible futures for the village of Ford. Is Ford dying, as some observers believe? Or are there signs of vitality which suggest a healthy community life for the indefinite future?

We cannot expect the evidence to be clear-cut and decisive. It is impossible to be objective, precise, and quantitative in weighing the facts. We can, on the other hand, attempt to discern, by looking for the presence of vital signs, which of the possible alternative futures seems most likely.

Futures for Ford

There are, I believe, three possible directions for the village of Ford. From looking at the trends of the past decade or so, one could reasonably project an optimistic future—one in which Ford's population increases and its age structure does not grow older, one in which Ford enjoys a stable economic base and works toward collective ends through institutionalized activities grounded in a shared sense of place.

Alternatively, from looking at the community over the long sweep of history, one might just as reasonably project a continuation of the long-term decline in population and institutional vigour which began in the early nineteenth century. Ford could follow many other Highland villages into oblivion. It could disappear from the map, and after a generation or two, there would be few to mourn its passing.

The third possibility is that Ford might hold on to life by a thread; that it might enter a state of dying and remain there 'vegetating', as it were, indefinitely. Its institutions and collective patterns may become weakened. Its conflicts and divisions could become heightened. Shared identity and commitment to place could fade. The capacity for localized decision-making could be lost almost entirely. All these things could happen, gradually, imperceptibly, and yet enough could remain of the population and of the 'vital signs' to support some minimal form of human association. Slow death could well develop into an enduring pattern of association as it has for many other communities in the world which are hardly alive but which refuse to die.

My own conclusion, which I will state at the outset, is that there are enough signs of vitality in Ford to render a reasonably favourable prognosis. It seems doubtful, at least, that Ford will die out altogether, although, as we shall see, its future is really not in its own possession. Let us look first at the evidence favouring this relatively optimistic conclusion of survival before then turning to some inescapable qualifications.

The evidence for optimism lies partly in the figures discussed in the last chapter, which show a well-defined increase in population over the past fifteen years. The data there show that while depopulation has not ceased (and will probably continue to take away many young people), its effects have been offset by the numbers of recent incomers, most of whom are *not* retirees. Not only has the number of people increased, but the population appears to be growing slightly younger. The increase in numbers of people has meant an increase in new and improved housing—and not just for retirement couples.

Nor is the local economy dying. A substantial number of individuals appear to be making a decent living from hill farming in and around Ford. Agriculture is anything but dying when a total of over 17,000 acres is being farmed, supporting 4,250 sheep, 244 cows, 12 men, 10 women, and 21 children. Forty-three of Ford's 156 inhabitants are in farm families.

The same can be said of forestry and timber work. While the number of forestry-related workers may be declining, the industry still involves a large number of people in Ford: a total of 23 men, women, and children are in families supported by timber and forestry-related occupations. At least one man, Joachim Brolly, has found opportunities for rapid expansion in the timber business, and says he could hire more than sixty new men 'tomorrow' if they could be found.

A village is not asleep or dying when a sizeable majority of its people are engaged in one or another collective activity which benefits the whole. The Village Hall may be less used than it was when it was the new pride of the community, but it is nevertheless in regular use for community affairs, and it was a lively place on the last Saturday of November 1981 when almost one hundred people crowded into it for a sale of work to benefit the forthcoming children's Christmas party. The Ford Gun Club, the SWRI, and Hall Committee are also still quite active.

A community is alive when its people are designing new enterprises and implementing new schemes which promise work for its members. Two fish farms (one unsuccessful), two nurseries, and a timber business have been started in and around Ford in the last ten years. People have shown strong imagination in creating work where there was none before: one man is a privately contracting deerstalker, apparently the only one in the West Highlands; another earns his income through a combination of various teaching jobs and his own painting. Another new fish-farming scheme seems to be aborning, this one, significantly, to be organized on a cooperative basis. Ford does not seem to me to be a place where most people are apathetic and have gone to sleep. It is alive and awake, and in its midst there are those who intend to keep it that way.

Quite aside from the issue of collective activities and shared institutional patterns as signs of community vitality, there is the question of shared identity which is place-related. This issue is especially critical in Ford where place-related identity could be undermined easily, if unintentionally, by the large number of recent incomers. It is possible to imagine a Ford which enjoys a reasonable population, the jobs to support it, the forms of social life and the amenities required to sustain village life, but a Ford which is nevertheless hollow, lacking in soul and shared identity. It is important, therefore, to ask what sense of place exists in Ford now, whether is is shared, and how it is likely to change.

The subject of 'sense of place' does not seem to have been given much attention by analysts, whether philosophers or social scientists.[4] Relph points out that:

> Place and sense of place do not lend themselves to scientific analysis for they are inextricably bound up with all the hopes, frustrations, and confusions of life, and possibly because of this social scientists have avoided these topics.[5]

In attempting to deal with the topic himself, Relph suggests some provocative, if unproven, principles. To have attachment to places and feel deep ties with them are important human needs, he says, agreeing with Robert Coles, whom he quotes:

> Nations, regions, states, counties, cities, towns—all of them have to do with politics and geography and history; but they are more than that, for they somehow reflect man's humanity, his need to stay someplace and get to know . . . other people . . . and what I suppose can be called a particular environment or space or neighbourhood or set of circumstances.[6]

Relph and Coles both seem to feel that the attachment to place need not grow out of lifelong location in a single place, but from 'settings in which we have had a multiplicity of experiences and which call forth an entire complex of affections and responses'. Relph, following Heidigger and Vycinas, distinguishes between levels of attachment to place, using 'home' to describe the deepest level of connection, for 'home' is where one dwells, the place where one's being and identity begin. It is the 'point of departure from which we orient ourselves to the world'.[7]

The identities of places can come about in two ways, says Relph; they can grow naturally as people unselfconsciously come to share common knowledge of features and values associated with a locality, or they can be 'mass identities' (C. Wright Mills' term) created by image-makers and marketed as saleable images of localities, such as Disneyland, which are really pseudoplaces based on synthetic identities and stereotypes.[8] The ultimate in placelessness occurs when powerful central authority, or big business, or mass culture, in the grip of a faceless economic system weakens the identity of a site through surface, stereotypical messages which finally make all places look alike and 'offer the same bland possibilities for experience'.[9]

In Ford, a very strong sense of place is expressed by most of the residents, whether they are incomers, natives, or long-term residents. (The exceptions, including the few who said they would really prefer to be some place else, did not fall into any *one* of these categories.) To evoke statements about place, I asked a number of different questions: What does Ford mean to you? How do you describe it to people from some place else? What do you like about it and dislike about it? What makes it unique or the same as other places? Would you prefer to be some place else? Where would you like to be buried? And, of incomers, what brought you to Ford?

The most commonly expressed imagery of Ford involves scenery, quiet country living, rainy weather, local history, trees, sheep, and people (variously characterized as friends, family, neighbours, or just 'my people'). Some examples:

I asked a long-term resident if she had ever thought of living elsewhere. She wouldn't move, she said, even if there were an alternative to Ford. She did not want an alternative; she was quite content with this place. Her sources of contentedness were her friends, her part-time job which put her in frequent association with friends. 'I'm in a rut, I suppose,' she said, 'but I'm contented. I don't even want to go on holiday. If I lived somewhere else, I would miss my friends, and the place—my rut.'

Her son is attending a university in the south. When he is at school, he says, he misses the vistas, and he is always glad to get back to 'my people'. Asked to explain what 'my people' meant, he said, 'The people I grew up with, and to whom I enjoy returning with small triumphs.' But the place as place was just as important as the people, and the scenery and the weather were cited as major elements of it.

The elder Mr Murray explains that the family had never before visited Ford when they heard the hotel was for sale, but they liked what they saw and came to love the place. He said, 'Why live anywhere else when you can live here? We aren't making money, but it is a good life. The hours are long, but we close the hotel in the winter and have the place to ourselves. Everyone needs time to himself.' He has never considered moving anywhere else, because Ford has everything he and his family want. He once remarked that when he took a trip to America, what he missed most was seeing the sheep.

A Glasgow man who came into the area in 1958 to work for the Forestry Commission says he loves the simple life and the hardship. Although, he says, many others left after only two months, he stayed on. He does not want any more improvements brought here. He says it would spoil his life.

Another Glasgow man who just moved to Ford with his wife chose this as the place to retire because it reminded him most of the West Highland area as he knew it when he travelled it on business years ago. 'It has changed the least. Most other places in Scotland have new high rises or have built up in new directions. I took a picture on the Crinan Canal in 1932 and it looks just the same today. There have been too many changes in other places.'

A woman who used once to come to Dalavich on holidays eventually married a man from there, and they moved to Ford in 1973. She likes the general area because it is quiet and because 'everyone minds their own business'. She likes Ford better than Dalavich because it is closer to Lochgilphead. What she does not like about it is the lack of things to interest teenagers. And the weather. (She seems unusual in this respect. Most people seem to have a perverse affection for the rain in Argyll, which is just as well considering the 80 inches they see every year. There are standard lines about the wet weather just as there are standard greetings for everyday interaction. One person will say, 'Terrible day'. Another will say, 'Aye, well, it keeps the dust down.' And another will say, 'Aye, well, it's drier in here than it is out there.')

A retired Forestry Commission worker likes Ford because it has mild winters and he can be close enough to a town without having to live in one. ('I don't like cities—they're all go,' says his wife.) He would not want to leave Ford, although, ironically, his wife, who is one of the few natives in Ford, would really prefer to live in a slightly larger village because of the conveniences. But he would miss the people in Ford, and he would miss working on the land, which he still does occasionally. She says she would miss the friends she meets daily in her work, although, she adds, people have changed and there is not the friendliness there once was.

An 85-year-old woman who moved to Ford with her late husband in 1939 admitted that she wasn't satisfied with her life here at first. 'I didn't like it. It was so quiet, and so far away from my home (near the Kyles of Bute). But we got settled down in it and had many a happy day. We made good friends. We never lived anywhere else; this is where our good friends are.' She is not certain the village will be so friendly a place in the future.

Another couple has been here since 1925. They had no special feeling for the place at first because it was 'a continuation of what we always had—just a country place.' The man has travelled extensively in his seventy-nine years. He says he has never had any 'great notion to move anyplace else. When I lose the hills I'm away from home.'

An older Scottish couple chose to return to Ford for their retirement because 'We really belong here. My family has been here for generations.' They have lived in the country and farmed nearby all their lives. The wife admits that she would like to be nearer to Lochgilphead because the shopping is better, some of her friends are there, and it is closer to a main bus route. But this is home. They plan to be buried in Kilmartin cemetery, which is the closest to Ford.

An English couple who retired here years ago describe themselves as 'born Londoners' who nonetheless have made a strong commitment to Ford as their new home. Most people, he observes, say they want to live in the place where they enjoy their holidays, and that is what this couple did, although not until they had spent considerable time here getting to know the place and the people. They describe it as 'still a holiday'. 'We have everything here to please the eye and enchant the senses.' They are ardent conservationists and work for the preservation of the natural beauty of the area. They question the desirability of bringing new industry in: 'Do we want industry brought to keep the young here?' This couple has been active in community organizations, but their sense of place is, in the main, rooted in the things that 'please the eye and enchant the senses'. Because his family originated in Lewis and spent some time in Argyll, the husband likes to imagine there is some ancient racial memory of the place deep within him: 'It's almost an instinctive feeling. I'm a different person when I'm in the south and when I'm here.'

Another, more recently arrived, retired English family says that nostalgia and family feeling brought them to Scotland. They feel they have been well received by the people of Ford. But it is really the *place* that attracts and holds them, judging from statements like, 'When I return here, I see these hills beside the loch, and I think, "These are *my* hills."' Sentiments such as this suggest a deep commitment to place has developed in a relatively short time.

For another recent incomer, whose work in timber brought him here, Ford seems to be just a place where the work is. Working 16-hour days seven days a week, this man doesn't participate in community activities. He finds that 'Drink's a curse on this part of the world' and therefore would not participate in pub life if he had the time. Ford is a good place to bring up boys because of the work in forestry it affords, but there is not much for girls, in his opinion. Because work is so important to this man, Ford as a place simply represents work to him.

For an older native single lady living at Torran in one of the renovated flats, Ford is a place filled with memories and ghosts. She recalls that her very sitting room was once the tool room for Torran Farm, and the bedroom was 'the bull's box'. The flat across from hers was the byre, the place where cattle were kept; she smiled wryly as she reflected on her seventy-three years in Ford: 'If

anyone had told me that I would ever be having tea in Torran byre ...'.
On the other hand, she has family elsewhere, and she visits them
frequently. She admits that because of the family ties elsewhere,
now that the brother with whom she lived in Ford is dead, she
'might not miss Ford' if she were to move. (I am not certain she is
right; ghosts and lifelong memories have a way of travelling, too.)

Even for a small place such as Ford, a locality can mean many
things to many people, but the most common themes which
emerged from my conversations with people were the physical and
aesthetic qualities of the area ('scenery'), a sense of its past
('history'), and a complex of associations with people ('friends').
For many, the Scottishness of the area was important enough to
mention, especially in the case of many English incomers. (No
doubt it would have registered as more important for the Scots as
well had not most of them taken it for granted.) For some of these
people, the land, the lore, and the history seemed to blend together
and their appreciation of the place was as a totality.

It might surprise some to learn how deep a sense of place is held
by some of the recent incomers. They spend time on the land, they
read about local history, they work toward its enhancement and
preservation. Ironically, I met one set of English incomers who
voted for Scottish devolution in 1979 and then discovered moments
later that members of the most Scottish of Scots families in Ford
had voted *against* the measure, which would have granted greater
independence from Westminster to Scotland. In other words, some
of the English families in Ford have become more self-consciously
'Scottish' than many of their born-Scots counterparts.

In addition, some of the incomers seem to be more attached to
Ford than a few of the natives, some of whom mentioned their
desire to live closer to 'the towns', even if it meant leaving Ford and
their friends behind. The lesson to be learned is, I think, that sense
of place, and the strength of that sentiment, are not *always* born out
of lifelong associations and memories of place and people. That
human need for a sense of place, for rootedness, can be so strong
that we sometimes, when the circumstances are proper, sink our
roots deeply in a very short time. This is apparently what has
happened with some of the incomers to Ford, and even some,
although perhaps not all, of the commuters.

So the question of how deep the sense of place is in Ford can be answered: very. This statement may seem stark in view of the qualification which is necessarily placed around it: the feelings of *some* individuals about the place are in fact shallow. But even though we cannot test it at this point in any quantitative way, the generalization appears reasonably accurate. And to a surprising degree, the elements of place which people cite as important or meaningful seem to be fairly consistent, even if not uniform. For most of the people of the village, whether they be native, long-term resident, or recent incomer, and whether they be Scottish or English, Ford is a place for which they feel affection and about which they care. With some exceptions among the commuters, most of their friends are here. They enjoy the surroundings and many cultivate a knowledge of local history and lore. It is a place where people are inclined to let their roots sink in. They make of it more than just a place to park. Being native, or having a long history of associations with the people and the surroundings provides excellent soil for the growth of roots, but the humus of accumulated years is not the only medium in which roots grow into place. The finding of good new friends and the closeness to land, history, and things that 'enchant the senses' seem to be sufficient for many. And some, I suspect, are in love only with the 'differentness' of the place and culture, especially if they are tied to former home environments, which many are. It will be ironic if this affection results in so tight an embrace that the life is squeezed from indigenous culture, but this is a process which often accompanies rural gentrification.

A place does not have to be objectively unique and distinct from all other places in order for a strong sense of identity to grow around it. Very small differences—a minor physical feature, an historical event of no great import, some imagined difference in the character of the people—can be taken and made into exaggerated qualities, unique meanings, distinguishing symbols of a whole complex of otherwise very ordinary traits and features. Such differences can become the basis of identity-related beliefs about a place and its people. ('Our people aren't like the people of nearby X. X community is just a totally different place from Y community.')

Ford's people share such a sense of uniqueness. It is expressed in their interest in local history, and in the amount of time people like to spend out-of-doors, on the land, in the hills, on the water, and with each other.

Given these expressions about place, I reach the conclusion that there is a strong shared identity related to locality among the villagers of Ford. Part of feeling rooted is a concomitant caring about place, and as long as people care about a place as much as people in Ford do, it will remain more than just a population—it will be a living community.

The question of relative autonomy—the extent to which the village exercises authority over decisions which affect it—is perhaps the most critical in weighing its future. Those matters over which the people of Ford *can* exercise control are in fact influenced by them, but the truth is that the future of Ford depends primarily on circumstances over which it has no control. For although this fact does not often bore into the consciousness of the villagers, Ford is a tiny part of a vast world economy. It is not even the tail wagged by the dog; it is merely a hair on that tail. Moreover, the dog does not live anywhere near Scotland, let alone Ford.

The point deserves elaboration because, like so many of these observations, what is true for Ford seems also to be true for most small communities worldwide.

It is entirely accurate to say that Ford is peripheral, but it is not the isolated place the summer visitor believes it to be. (I recall a Dutch couple who strayed into the Ford Hotel for overnight lodging. They thought places like Ford were marvellous; they expressed pleased astonishment that people in places like this did not read newspapers or watch television. They thought it incredibly quaint that Ford could ignore the rest of the world and live as it did a hundred years before. I was unable to penetrate this wholly imaginary view of Highland life. They would not look when I tried to call their attention to the stack of newspapers at the end of the bar. They did not hear the monotony of the television in the next room. They came for the scenery, for the local colour, to enjoy that figment of the imagination the Scottish Tourist Board calls 'Scotland', and they would not allow reality to intrude on their holiday.)

Indeed, because Ford *is* on the periphery, but is *not* isolated, it is less able to influence the decisions made in faraway places upon which much of its vitality hinges.

Major Warde-Aldam points out, for example, that the continuation of agriculture in the area depends in large part on government policies. Dependent as farmers are on UK subsidies and EEC 'Hill Livestock Compensatory Allowances,' it is easy to see his point. Economic philosophies come and go as political parties take turn about in government; who is there to guarantee hill farming subsidies for the indefinite future? If all the Fords in the Highlands conspired to block vote, and if they persuaded their Lowland Scots cousins to join with them—a feat which no one expects to see in this millennium—they could still be out-voted ten to one by people living on the other side of the Cheviot Hills. And if the United Kingdom spoke with one voice, it would be one among many in the Common Market, where policies affecting the Highlands are frequently hammered out.

Moreover, the presence of the HIDB has been a constant in the social and economic environment of the Highlands for over fifteen years. It has pumped millions of dollars into the development of enterprises and cultural and social amenities over this period of time, amounting to about $350 per man, woman, and child in the Highlands in the first eighteen years of its existence.[10] But the HIDB was a creation of a Labour government which is no longer in power. It is, according to one HIDB staff member, regarded with suspicion by landowners and businesses in the region who sometimes worry about its sweeping powers. For all the good it has done in the region, a government hungry for budget cuts may look closely at its budget, despite its relatively small size. The appointment as Chairman of a non-Highland Conservative, whose most recent experience was in Hong Kong, has raised a question about the government's plans for the HIDB. As in other areas of government practice and policy, the people of areas such as Ford have little to say in the matter.

Similarly, Ford influences neither the world market nor the domestic markets for sheep, cattle, venison, fish, nursery plants, timber, tourist services, or any of the other products and services upon which the livelihoods of its residents depend. It is, instead, at their mercy.

Increasingly, the tourist market is moving from the hands of small local entrepreneurs to urban-based companies and government agencies. While the Scottish Tourist Board does work diligently to bring in foreign tourists, it does so by the use of inane and inauthentic imagery, as though Scotland were nothing but scenery and bagpipes, employing, for example, the highly inappropriate Larry Hagman (inappropriate not because he is Mr Hagman but because he is better known as the fictional J.R. Ewing of US television fame) to sell the 'product'. Large tour bus companies are buying up hotels in the Highlands so that they can package their tours more dependably, efficiently, and cheaply through controlling all the elements of the system—transportation, accommodations, and meals. The consequence is to place the smaller hotels and guest houses at a competitive disadvantage because the buses will not bring passengers to them anymore.

One small example from Ford illustrates the centralization of the tourist business into larger, more heavily capitalized businesses. On my second visit to the village, my wife and I met a young woman from Edinburgh in the Ford Hotel where we were all enjoying a bar lunch. She was in Ford as part of her job, which involves travelling throughout Scotland, mostly in the Highlands, looking at prospective listings for her agency and reporting on them. She represented a private company in Edinburgh which books holiday home rentals, brokering between prospective tenants and property owners. In short, even bookings into small private guest homes are becoming centralized.

Whether families continue to move into the area as they have been doing for the past few years will depend not so much on what Ford does as it will upon such imponderables as the continuation of urban flight, the pervasiveness of back-to-the-land philosophies, the availability and cost of property in Ford compared with other areas, and the general state of the economy. Rural property in the Highlands and the way of life it is thought to represent are being made commodities which are very marketable at the moment. Agents in Edinburgh, Glasgow, and London will be much better prophets of this market than anyone in Ford. For the time being, estate agents and solicitors in Lochgilphead and Oban are enjoying a brisk business.

The kinds of people who come to Ford to live in the future will depend on the availability of work, the convenience of transportation for commuters, and availability of services and amenities, the quality of education, and so on. They will depend in part also on the preservation of the natural beauty of the surroundings and the maintenance of the peaceful, 'easy-osy' atmosphere sought by many urban refugees today. But the creation of jobs and the control of all the other factors which influence decisions to move in or stay are the result of more than just local initiative.

The future of Ford also depends on its relationship to the town of Lochgilphead. This is true both because there are jobs there for people to commute to from Ford, and also because what people in Lochgilphead think of Ford will help make it what it becomes. If Lochgilphead continues its pattern of growth as an employment centre, and if transportation costs do not continue to escalate excessively, then the nearby villages, including Ford, could continue to receive the population overflow. But the connection between Ford and Lochgilphead depends to some degree on how the planners, estate agents, and decision-makers view it. If they believe that Ford is too far away, or that it is not a 'defined village', or that it is a disappointing place to which to send prospective buyers of property, then the demise of Ford could become a self-fulfilling prophecy.

All of these matters—government policies regarding agriculture, forestry, tourism, and the HIDB; the whims of the marketplace; the attitudes of prospective incomers toward the advantages and costs of country living; the availability of work; and the connection to Lochhilphead and its fortunes—are unknowns in the equation by which Ford's tomorrows will be calculated.

While the connections between a peripheral area such as Ford and the centres of political and economic power can be traced, it is not possible to predict or prophesy changes in policy and influence which might emanate from these centres in the future. But my assessment is that unless there is some surprising development, or unless all the 'unknowns' take negative turns simultaneously in some cumulative way, Ford's future is relatively sound. It has more than an even chance of life.

On the other hand, the argument that Ford might die, or that it will vegetate indefinitely, is a plausible one. Any optimistic conclusion must be tempered with the knowledge that there are signs of dying as well as signs of life. What is the nature of this negative evidence?

There is, first, the long-term downward drift in population. This drift has been of too long duration and is too widespread throughout the West Highlands to be ignored. It is possible, for example, that the recently experienced increase in residents is merely an isolated spike on a long, down-slipping demographic line. If the best guide to the future is the pattern of the past, then decline may well continue over the long term.

There are signs of ill health in the village itself, matters which have not escaped the notice or concern of its residents. Some of these signs have directly to do with the indicators of dying and vitality discussed earlier, especially that regarding institutional patterns. One such sign, for example, is the closing of the Ford school in 1972.

The community rallied late in the day to save its school, but its closing was a foregone conclusion given the small numbers of pupils in attendance and the government's need to contain the costs of education throughout the country. The school was one of the centres of community life and pride. Parents of children who once attended it have told me repeatedly how much it meant to them and how much they miss even the small things associated with it, such as hearing the children playing in the schoolyard, or watching them collect on the bridge on their way to the school house: they could visualize the future of their world in the collectivity of Ford's youth. Now the children are taken away by van daily and schooled elsewhere.

There are practical as well as nostalgic concerns about the closing of the school, reflected in the thoughts of Kathy Mac-Dougall about what could become of Ford:

> It could become a derelict village. I think a community loses a lot when it loses its school. When families think about coming in, they will look for a school for their children. Compare Ford with Clachan, which fought for its school and now has a two-teacher school.

The closing of the school may represent more than just the loss of an important institutional pattern in Ford. The lack of success in resisting the closure could also be said to represent some weakness in the ability of the village to engage in collective action at a critical time when the community's interests were at stake. Nevertheless, the village did organize itself, which is a more important sign than the fact that it lost.

As we have already seen, Ford may also lose its church. The possibility of its closing is viewed with anxiety, not only by its few remaining communicants, but even by some of those who seldom or never occupy its pews. It could be said that much of what was vital about the church has already been lost; its contribution to community life was certainly greater when the minister could give it more of his attention and play a more active part in the village. To a certain extent, the closing of the church would be only a symbolic loss, but it is an important symbol to many nonetheless. And it is a centre of activity in the community for some, for whom it is even more important.

Nell Kerr put the matter well. She felt the closing of the school was a 'tragedy' and she now fears for the church. 'I think,' she said, 'that once the school goes and the church goes, the village will have a hard time laying the foundations of a good community life.'

Some segments of the economy upon which Ford's employment, income, and well-being depend have shown signs of weakness in recent times. Although Joachim Brolly and some of the other private timber contractors are either prospering or holding their own, the Forestry Commission continues to decrease the number of workers it employs. The timber industry is in a state of some confusion currently,[11] and there is discussion in government circles about 'denationalizing' the Forestry Commission itself in some way. The chief forester for Inverliever believes local forestry employment may decrease both because of the introduction of new machinery (a loader called a 'forwarder', which can load twenty-four hours a day and accomplish more in a few hours than existing machines can in a week) and because the Commission is not likely to purchase new land for planting. The forester thinks the centre of gravity has definitely shifted away from Ford as far as the Commission's work is concerned. 'Ford is a pity,' he said, 'It used to be the centre of the Forest.'

Tourism is another economic segment important to Ford and the work patterns of its residents. It has taken a downturn, beginning in the late nineteen-seventies. Whether because of fuel costs, unemployment, inflation, or the greater attraction of alternatives, fewer people are said to be touring Scotland these days, and the farther from the major cities (primarily Edinburgh), the greater the reduction of tourist traffic. As a consequence, the Ford Hotel has seen fewer of its beds filled over the last few years, and fewer anglers seem to come to Ford every year.

Not only has the number declined, but the nature of the touring population seems to have altered somewhat as well. Other resort areas in Britain have noted the same shift from a clientele made up of 'a better class of people' in earlier decades to one consisting of middle class and working class people today. The more prosperous visitors of earlier days were good for the hotel business because they enjoyed the 'catered' style of living as a part of their accustomed class privileges. When for a variety of reasons holiday-making became more popular among the less prosperous, it was affordable to them only if they 'catered' themselves or found other, less costly holiday accommodations. The boom in bed and breakfast homes was one consequence of this class shift in tourism. In Ford, the bed and breakfast wave arrived only recently; the only two such guest houses which exist were introduced within the last six years. The presence of these guest houses does not appear to have drained an appreciable number of visitors away from the Ford Hotel, although they may have had some effect. The two are not precisely in competition with each other because of the appeal to different types of clientele. Nevertheless, the rise of one type of accommodation and the simultaneous decline of the other signals a class shift in the consumers of Scottish holidays. Many of the 'better class' choose to jet to foreign countries these days, perhaps just because the Scottish Highlands are so much more accessible to the middle and working classes.

The presence of 'self-catering' visitors has two other consequences for Ford. One is the increased number of dwellings owned by non-residents who occupy them only a few weeks out of the year. Some of these are strictly holiday homes, second homes of city dwellers who visit Ford only on certain weekends or on two-week or one-month holidays. Others are intended as retirement homes, used meanwhile as holiday homes. The second consequence is the erection of small mobile homes on the lochside by farmers who leave them parked there year-round and rent them during the summer to self-catering visitors. There were 26 such mobile homes on the southeast side of Loch Awe in autumn, 1981, most of them shabby old camping trailers (caravans) occupied by temporary urban refugees who add little to either the local economy or the scenery. (In fact, their despoilation of the scenery will no doubt bring further decline to the tourist business around Loch Awe.)

When one looks at the decline of certain institutional patterns such as the school and the church, the precariousness of work patterns associated with forestry and tourism, and the possibility of long-term population declines, any optimistic projection of Ford's future must be qualified and cautious. Nor can one help but be more pessimistic about the future after listening to certain outsiders who are familiar with the community. The minister, for example, thinks the population will continue to diminish:

> There are some new bungalows in Ford, yes, but it is not likely to receive further depopulation from Lochgilphead. It is not a dying community, but . . . .
> Unless something happens out of the blue, I can't imagine it increasing. All but four families at Kilmartin are retired families. Ford is getting to be that kind of community. It's not really at this stage now because there are some employed with the Forestry Commission. But that appears to be the situation.

The minister's impressions may not be entirely accurate, but, whatever his basis, his forecast is one of decline.

Likewise, a physical planner with the Argyll and Bute District Council in Lochgilphead sees no growth ahead for Ford. The overflow from Lochgilphead, as long as it lasts, will be sopped up by closer-by Kilmichael and eventually by Kilmartin, says the planner, but not by Ford, which is too far away. Besides, to use the planner's inimitable language,

> Ford, bless its cotton socks, is not quite a defined village like Kilmichael, or even Kilmartin. It won't disappear, but there's not likely to be any more pressure for building in Ford.

One gets the impression that Ford has been written off by the government planners as well as by the minister and the forester.

Not only outsiders, but some of its residents, too, offer gloomy forecasts. Not all are pessimistic, but those who are seem to feel that the place is rapidly becoming transformed into a retirement village with no future unless new retirees replace old ones as the latter die off. One says it is an 'elderly community', another believes it will become 'an old folks' home', and another is worried about too many 'non-breeders' in the population. And I recall again my first conversation in the village when a resident characterized Ford as dying, saying that it would soon become a deserted ghost village filled with ruins like others in the area.

I find all these dismal prophecies exaggerated, however. Some are based on limited personal experience, some on misinformation, some on old information which does not bring the story of Ford up to date. My answer to the question: Will Ford survive? is a qualified 'Yes'. I see signs of continuing life in the village. I think it will continue indefinitely as a living, not a dying community. But I think it will change socially and culturally. Indeed, I believe that much of the pessimism of residents about the future has in fact been caused by the confusion of *change* with *death*.

Winds of Change

Ford has turned a corner in its long history and is not likely to be any of the things it has been in its previous eras. It will change culturally, the structures of social life will alter, and new divisions will continue to cut across it.

How is Ford changing now and what will it become like? A reasonable conjecture can be made from understanding the kinds of demands and wants which will be made by the new population mix of the village. Such a social-demographic analysis would suggest that there will be increasing pressure for more readily available services and services of high quality. Fortunately, good health care can already be found in Lochgilphead, where there are doctors, nurses, and regional hospitals. There may, however, be an increasing demand for services related to home health care. Likewise, because there are numerous school-age children in the new population, parents will be concerned with school issues such as educational quality, transportation, safety, and the like. And although library services improved in the nineteen-sixties, they are seen as inadequate by some of the people of Ford. In general, because many of the new incomers arrive from cities and are accustomed to the convenience and entertainments of urban living, they will carry some of these expectations with them despite the fact that they came to a place like Ford to escape from the city. They would like, as most of us would, to enjoy the serenity, personal friendliness, and pastoral qualities of country living without sacrificing the conveniences of town living. The geologist misses access to books, the wife of a forester misses shopping in large stores, a retired couple miss having the full range of electrical appliances, and the young people miss the dances, the movies, the record shops. The wants and tastes of the urbanized incomers will continue to be felt as pressure for improved services generally.

In a similar vein, we have seen already what kinds of effects the new population of Ford has on community organizations. It is an exaggeration to say (as a few in Ford do) that the incomers have taken over, but they have played a strong role in carrying on existing organizations and in innovating new ones. As numerous villagers point out, the incomers bring 'fresh blood and new ideas' to Ford. This innovative spirit is likely to continue as long as there are incomers (and it is just as likely to engender some of the resentment presently found among some of the longer-term residents). It is even conceivable that newcomers could become more involved in the church, if it is granted a reprieve and its mission is rejuvenated. The experiences that people bring with them of activities and organizations in other locales will have some effect on the structures of social life in Ford; new ideas will be experimented with, and some will be discarded while others become institutionalized.

On the other hand, there is a large element of the population of recent incomers which does not participate much in the organization or social life of the village. If Ford becomes a 'bedroom' community for more commuters, the proportion of non-participants may grow. Still, the recruitment of people to voluntary associations is usually a struggle in most communities, and the pattern in Ford may not be so different, or become so different, from elsewhere.

It is likely that the hotel pub will continue to be an important focus of village life, but it may become a place where the new divisions in the community become more visible. Going to the pub is a cultural pattern more familiar to natives and less recent Scottish incomers; it seems to attract younger persons and those whose work is in or near Ford more than it attracts commuters, older persons, English incomers, and those whose family life appears to absorb all their attention. There is something very Scottish about the pub, and there is no reason to believe that this cultural atmosphere will weaken. And if more people work outside the village, it is probable that fewer will feel they have time to spend in leisurely evenings at the pub. The focus of life for a number of these new people—the commuters—will be work and family.

What will the role of the estates be in the future of Ford? Our earlier history of the estates surrounding Ford makes it clear that they were much more important in its past than they are at the present time. I once asked Robin Malcolm of Poltalloch how he thought the relationship of the laird to the local community had changed. In his answer, he dated much of the change from just before World War Two. The changes are rather dramatic: the laird used to be the local authority, deciding where and when and how schools, churches, and houses would be built. Now these decisions are in the hands of local authorities, selected public bodies and the staffs appointed to assist them. In addition, at one time everyone in the village would have been working for the laird, and their services would have been let out to other users as their time was available and their skills in demand. Now, except for a handful, the villagers are independent of the laird's employment. Some aspects of the ancient feudal system still hold, but for the most part, the estate merely represents another large-scale landholding in the neighbourhood.

In the case of Ford, what has happened to the estates in the past has had direct influences on the nature of village life, as we have seen. There is presently only one major estate operating there. If Ederline were to be sold to an owner who chose not to farm it, or if government policies made farming infeasible, the economy and work patterns of Ford would be affected drastically. If the lands of

Ederline, Auchinellan, or Creaganterve were to be sold to the Forestry Commission, hill farming could virtually disappear, but such an event is unlikely under current government policies. If these estates were to be broken up and sold piecemeal for retirement, second-home, holiday or other residential purposes, again the farming sector of the local economy would be sharply affected. On the other hand, the resale of small portions of estate lands could lead to an increase in the incomer population.

The greatest likelihood is that estate lands in Ford will continue to be used for farming, no matter into whose hands they fall, as long as the EEC and UK government subsidies continue to make hill farming a break-even or marginally profitable activity. It is not likely that any imaginable changes in ownership patterns would alter the authority patterns between the estates and the village of Ford; as Robin Malcolm points out, those changes occurred years ago.

Ford will change culturally in subtle ways. Old customs and patterns are changing (as they always have been) to the extent that some feel a loss of culture even now. As more incomers arrive, especially urban people and non-Scots, new ideas and customs and habits arrive with them. What they do *not* bring is just as important. They do not bring with them a culture which duplicates what was there before—a replacement culture which fills in the missing elements lost as the natives leave or die. With a population as mobile as this one (over half the people in residence in 1981 having arrived within the previous 12 years), it would be difficult to imagine Ford duplicating itself culturally over even one generation. Even without the effect of incomers on local culture, ways of life in Ford are changing as a result of its connectedness with the world at large. The introduction of television is just one example.

It is therefore not surprising to hear people lament the passing of ceilidhs. Many of the individuals who contributed their talents are now dead, and many of the newcomers, although they enjoy the consumption of Scottish music, story-telling, and dancing, cannot furnish these talents themselves. And even many of the natives would, one suspects, be tempted to stay home and watch television. Nor is it so surprising to hear that most people now knock before entering someone else's home; this is the product of urban ways displacing country ways. The old-timers say that nothing is safe from theft anymore, and this is a lamentable fact, one which again results from high mobility, increased closeness to towns and cities, and the presence of more strangers passing through. (As one man put it succinctly 'Glasgow has come too near us. Loch Awe has been flogged to death.') Perhaps it is true as well that the older pattern of 'visiting' has fallen off. An elderly widow opined that the new people tend 'to stay to themselves. They don't visit. That's the style of people they are.'

Thus is Ford changing and thus will Ford continue to change. It will be a different place in the future from what it is now, and people will continue to miss the ways of life with which they have become familiar in their lifetimes. But this is nothing new—Ford has always been changing, and it is easy to imagine the good folks of several generations ago lamenting the passing of the Gaelic (as they no longer do in Ford but do further north and in the Western Isles), the declining use of the drove road, or the disappearance of the horse.

Culture change is a normal, if saddening process. If it takes place at too fast a rate, it can produce tensions and dislocations which divide a community seriously. It could conceivably exacerbate the division which already exists in incipient form in the village of Ford. But it is possible for people to share the ingredients of a sense of place to a sufficient degree that differences in ways of life are tolerated, that new ways blend with old, and that a people can work through their tensions together. It remains to be seen whether Ford will accommodate its own differences on the one hand or fall into more separated segments on the other. Whether its sense of 'Scottishness' can be shared or whether it will be divisive seems to me a most critical issue.

The making and keeping of a community requires more than merely maintaining a population in a locality and providing them basic services. It requires that people representing political and economic authority outside the community become the authors of policies and programmes which nurture life and do not presume the death of small places. Moreover, a community, as contrasted with a mere population, cannot persist that does not nourish shared perceptions and basic values, shared experiences, a shared sense of place which manifests itself in shared activity and collective action on behalf of the whole.

Ford could die. There are sufficient signs of dying to cause concern. But it is living now and its vital signs could continue and grow stronger. The question facing Ford is whether it will devolve into a set of people living side by side, acting together only in emergencies, sharing only their surfaces, or whether it will continue—and will be encouraged by public policy and private initiatives—to be the community that it is now, 'laying the foundations of a good community life' for its inheritors.

Footnotes

[1]Art Gallaher, Jr. and Harland Padfield, 'Theory of the Dying Community', in Art Gallaher, Jr. and Harland Padfield, *The Dying Community* (Albuquerque: University of New Mexico, 1981,), pp. 1-22.

[2]In addition to several of the essays in Gallaher and Padfield, *op. cit.,* the works of Willis Sutton, Roland Warren, Kai Erikson, Joseph Gusfield. and Howard Newby have been highly useful to my thinking. See, foı example, Willis Sutton and Jiri Kolaja, 'Elements of Community Action', *Social Forces*, 38 (May 1960), 325-331; Willis Sutton and Jiri Kolaja, 'The Concept of Community', *Rural Sociology*, 25 (June 1960), 197-203; Roland L. Warren, 'The Good Community—What Would It Be?' *Journal of the Community Development Society*, 1 (Spring 1970), 14-23; Kai Erikson, *Everything in Its Path—Destruction of Community in the Buffalo Creek Flood* (New York: Simon and Schuster, 1976), esp. the concluding chapter, pp. 246-259; Joseph R. Gusfield, *Community—A Critical Response* (New York: Harper and Row, 1975); Howard Newby, *Social Change in Rural England* (Madison: University of Wisconsin Press, 1979).

[3]Art Gallaher, Jr., 'Dependence on External Authority and the Decline of Community', in Gallaher and Padfield, *op. cit.,* 85-108.

[4]One exception is the interesting and helpful essay by anthropologist Judith Ennew entitled, 'Self Image and Identity in the Hebrides' (in Anthony Jackson, ed., *Way of Life and Identity*, Social Science Research Council, North Sea Oil Occasional Paper No. 4, n.d., circa 1980, pp. 49-

62). Professor Ennew describes four relatively distinct constructs of identity: those of the State, Academia, Tourism, and Self-Image. I am concerned with the last of these sources of image and identity in this section.

[5]Edward Relph, *Place and Placelessness* (London: Pion Limited, 1976), Preface.

[6]Quoted in Relph, *op. cit.*, p. 38.

[7]*Ibid.*, p. 43.

[8]*Ibid.*, pp. 58-9.

[9]*Ibid.*, p. 90.

[10]HIDB, 'The Highlands and Islands, A Contemporary Account' (Inverness: February 1979), p. 102.

[11]James Hunter, 'Taking Root: The Strangest Export Trade in Scotland' *Sunday Standard* (September 27, 1981), p. 17.

Appendix

Table 1: Numbers of Cattle and Sheep, Argyll, Selected Years from 1919 to 1975

Table 2: Total Acres under Plantation by Forestry Commission Inverliever, Inverinan, and Eredine Forests Combined, Selected Years, 1925-1980

Table 3: Number of Forest Workers Employed in Scotland, 1954-1979, West Scotland, 1971-1979, and for the United Kingdom, 1921-22 to 1949-50, for Selected Years

Table 4: Number of Persons Employed on Agricultural Holdings, Argyll, Selected Years, 1937-1978

Table 5: Number of Agricultural Holdings, Argyll, Selected Years from 1920 to 1975

Table 6: Number of Households and Number of Persons in Ford by Nationality and Nativity of Head, 1981

Appendix Table 1

Numbers of Cattle and Sheep, Argyll, Selected Years from 1919 to 1975

Year	No. of Cattle	No. of Sheep
1919	60,590	759,604
1920	58,162	776,818
1938	47,340	669,126
1945	59,552	683,543
1950	63,503	728,163
1955	63,796	706,360
1967	81,626	797,744
1970	86,260	738,757
1975	98,032	677,760

Source: *Agricultural Statistics, Scotland*

Appendix Table 2

Total Acres under Plantation by Forestry Commission, Inverliever, Inverinan, and Eredine Forests Combined, Selected Years, 1925-1980

Year	Area under Plantation, Three Forests Combined	Inverliever Only
1925	75	75
1935	296	114
1938	366	200
1945	49	—
1950	7,151	4,483
1955	10,570	5,898
1960	12,428	6,779
1965	15,118	7,331
1970	18,444	4,892
1975	27,542	18,718
1980	32,834	21,141

Source: Forestry Commission Reports

Appendix Table 3

Number of Forest Workers Employed in Scotland, 1954-1979,
West Scotland, 1971-1979, and for the United Kingdom,
1921-22 to 1949-50, for Selected Years

Year	United Kingdom	West Scotland	Scotland
1920-21	935	—	—
1929-30	3,835	—	—
1939-40	5,155	—	—
1944-45	5,070	—	—
1945-46	6,255	—	—
1949-50	12,100	—	—
1955	—	—	4,738
1960	—	—	4,105
1965	—	—	3,890
1970	—	—	2,965
1971	—	734	—
1975	—	568	2,375
1979	—	577	2,427

Sources: Forestry Commission Reports; *Scottish Abstract of
Statistics,* 1981.

Appendix Table 4

Number of Persons Employed on Agricultural Holdings, Argyll, Selected Years, 1937-1978

Year	No. Employed
1937	3,470
1938	3,338
1945	3,317
1950	3,205
1955	2,713
1967	1,531
1970	1,385
1975	1,270
1978	1,262

Source: *Agricultural Statistics, Scotland*

Appendix Table 5

Number of Agricultural Holdings, Argyll, Selected Years from 1920 to 1975

Year	No. of Holdings
1920	3,254
1938	3,054
1945	3,154
1950	3,156
1955	3,065
1967	2,385
1970	1,536
1975	1,339

Source: *Agricultural Statistics, Scotland*

Appendix Table 6

**Number of Households and Number of Persons in Ford
by Nationality and Nativity of Head, 1981**

No. in Household	Number of Households						Total	Total Persons
	Scottish		English		Irish	Native		
	Pre-1970	Post	Pre-1970	Post				
1	10	2			1	2	15	15
2	4	7	1	4		3	19	38
3	2	5		2			9	30
4	1	3		2		1	7	24
5		1	1	1	1	1	5	25
6	1	3					4	24
Total:	18	21	2	9	2	7	59	—
Total Persons:	34	65	7	27	6	17		156